The Washington Papers / 97   Volume XI

THE POLITICS OF ECONOMIC POLICY

France 1974–1982

VOLKMAR LAUBER

Foreword by Thibaut de Saint Phalle

Published with The Center for
Strategic and International Studies,
Georgetown University, Washington, D.C.

PRAEGER SPECIAL STUDIES • PRAEGER SCIENTIFIC

Library of Congress Cataloging in Publication Data

Lauber, Volkmar.
 The politics of economic policy, France 1974-1982.

 (The Washington papers, ISSN 0278-937X ; 97)
 "Published with the Center for Strategic and International Studies, Georgetown University, Washington, D.C."
 1. France—Economic policy—1945-   . I. Title.
 II. Series.
 HC276:2.L32 1983   338.944   83-2303
 ISBN 0-03-063423-7

The *Washington Papers* are written under the auspices of The Center for Strategic and International Studies (CSIS), Georgetown University, and published with CSIS by Praeger Publishers. The views expressed in these papers are those of the authors and not necessarily those of The Center.

Published in 1983 by Praeger Publishers
CBS Educational and Professional Publishing
a Division of CBS Inc.
521 Fifth Avenue, New York, New York 10175 U.S.A.

©1983 by The Center for Strategic and International Studies

All rights reserved

3456789 041 987654321

Printed in the United States of America

Contents

Foreword v

Introduction 1

I The Politics of Economic Policy under Giscard 5

    1. The Barre Policy: Rationale and Results 7
       Rationale 7
       Results 14

    2. The Political Environment: The Right 17

    3. The Political Environment: The Left 24

    4. Business and Labor 35

    5. Conclusion 43

II The Politics of Economic Policy under Mitterrand 47

6. Socialist Economic Policy 49

    From Reflation to Austerity 51
    Nationalization 53
    Policy toward the Private Sector 63

7. Social Reforms 68

    Redistribution of Income and Wealth 68
    Unemployment Policy 71
    Autogestion? 77

8. Problems and Prospects 79

    Dangers on the Left 81
    Dangers on the Right 87
    Political and Economic Viability 94

Notes 96

About the Author 120

Foreword

It is probably quite safe to say that Americans know less about French parliamentary politics than the French know about the workings of party politics and the Congress of the United States. Any careful study, therefore, of how the French political system operates and the relationship between labor unions and the political parties is of great interest to Americans concerned with U.S. policies toward Europe.

It has been said of the French that in France nothing is ever forgotten or forgiven. In politics this is true. You will find monarchists, Bonapartists, Trotskyists, anarchists—and all shades of opinion in between—among French politicians. Democracy has never come easily to the French. It came first through bloodshed in 1789, was lost to a military dictatorship and the panoply of a short-lived empire, was slowly developed again through the incapacity of successive returned monarchs, lost again to a new Napoleon, reborn in an endless stream of political pigmies both corrupt and inept—with a system designed to force compromise through which venality could reap its rewards. That France survived at all from the first to the so-called Fifth Republic must surely prove that government is not truly necessary.

Some years ago the then prime minister of Belgium met the newly designated prime minister of Italy at a European Commission meeting in Brussels. Said the Belgian Tindemans to Aldo Moro: "It must be very difficult to govern in your country. You seem to change governments continuously." "It is indeed difficult," replied Moro, "at times it seems almost impossible to govern Italy, but is it truly necessary?" One is often tempted to say the same of the French.

No one is more greatly admired in France than the queen of England. When President Kennedy was assassinated a pall settled on the country; farmers and workers put pictures of the late U.S. president on their walls. Yet the country has never had the same relationship with its own leaders—not even de Gaulle who did so much to recreate in postwar France a system of government that could combine a strong executive with parliamentary controls.

This study by Volkmar Lauber does not attempt to explain the strengths and deficiencies of a complex governmental structure. It does, however, carefully trace the flows of economic policy under President Giscard d'Estaing and his successor the current president, François Mitterrand. Because for the first time in a quarter century a government of the Left has succeeded to power in France, the change in policy has to be an exciting one, filled with philosophies of government not seen since Leon Blum was in power in 1937 trying to establish the Socialist counterpart of a Johnsonian Great Society in the face of Hitler's Germany across the Rhine. Indeed there are fascinating contradictions in this new attempt at socialism in France. A Socialist party with an absolute majority in Parliament, with a majority of this majority school teachers; a president who has vacillated over the course of his life from one end of the political spectrum to the other; a Cabinet that includes ministers from the extreme Left as well as others whom we might call Republican moderates. There is intelligence and passion as well as pragmatism here. There are men in this government who have already demonstrated an ability to grow in power and develop new ideas on the skeletons of old prejudices.

The author of this paper avoids bringing personalities to center stage, preferring to explain policies rather than focus on personalities. But his exposé is particularly pertinent in understanding how the new government has changed the economic direction in which the country is headed. He has given us a careful and complete presentation, and the relationship he traces between political personalities and labor leaders is particularly useful. He has not, however, indicated to us what will follow as a result of current failures in economic policy.

"Le plus ça change le plus c'est la même chose," says the French cynic. There is a feeling that the Socialist experiment in France is as doomed to failure as Reagan's attempt in the United States to balance the budget by sharp cuts in taxes accompanied by enormous increases in the military budget. Economically, this government will weaken France relative to West Germany as badly as Leon Blum's Socialist government did militarily in 1937. Both Reagan and Mitterrand believe in economic miracles: Reagan by reducing taxes while increasing the budget, Mitterrand by increasing wages and social benefits at a time when France is increasingly required to remain competitive.

It will be interesting to observe how in each country economic policies will be modified in due course to satisfy the needs of the country regardless of consideration of a particular political philosophy. Given the difference in political philosophy between Reagan and Mitterrand, this paper is all the more interesting.

> Thibaut de Saint Phalle
> Director, International
> Business and Economics, CSIS
>
> December 1982

Introduction

Since 1974, five major approaches have been tried out in an attempt to cope with the seemingly intractable problems of the French economy. Under President Valéry Giscard d'Estaing, a brief period of deflation was followed by an equally short period of reflation; this was followed by a period of stabilization. Then, in 1982, the Socialists made an effort to reflate again, while avoiding the pitfalls of such a policy. In addition, they undertook major changes in the distribution of income, wealth, and economic power. By mid-1982 reflation was abandoned, and a program of austerity plus public sector investments was introduced. Such "stop-go" policies are quite uncharacteristic of French economic management in the postwar period, and I will explore the conditions, political and economic, that led to the adoption of such policies.[1]

In the 1970s, in France as in many other industrial countries, the economy entered a troubled period. In fact, this trouble started in the 1960s, even if in retrospect that period is still one of comparative stability. But it was in the 1960s that the U.S. balance of payments problem began to fuel inflation in Europe significantly.[2] Several countries took measures to cope with this. In France one such measure was then Finance Minister Giscard's *plan de stabilisation*, which contributed to the explosion of 1968. International trade and monetary problems became increasingly serious in the early 1970s; inflation was on the rise in France and in many other countries. Yet for a time, the French government was remarkably successful in achieving its goals. The years of the Georges Pompidou presidency were marked by record growth rates, and even the balance of payments showed a slight surplus from 1970 to 1973.[3] Finally, unlike many other major industrial countries, France did not experience an important unemployment problem, and there was no decline in the rate of profit until 1973.[4]

The year 1974 marked the turning point. The quadrupling of oil prices and considerable increases in the prices of other raw materials created an important deficit in the balance of payments. At the same time, inflation (and thus interest rates) reached record levels. The first policy of Giscard, then newly elected president, was to deflate the French economy with his *plan de refroidissement* (cooling-off plan) of June 1974. It was thought that this would bring down interest rates, slow wage increases, and finally improve the balance of payments situation.

The immediate results were considerably worse than expected. Exports did stay ahead of imports, but economic growth fell below zero. The fall was particularly marked for industrial production.[5] Unemployment, which had been advancing slowly for some years, soared; investment, which had grown with great continuity over the preceding decade, suddenly collapsed.[6] Businesses sank still deeper into debt, and bankruptcies more than doubled.[7] But while in most major industrial countries wage increases slowed down, in France the progression of real wages continued at a rapid rate.[8] This was probably due to the narrow victory of Giscard over François Mitterrand in 1974.[9] In any case, the position of labor was strengthened in other ways as well, as when in late 1974 the government proposed a law providing for unemployment compensation at 90 percent of the previous salary for one year and expanded restrictions upon business that inhibited dismissals of wage earners at a time when production was falling and costs were rising.[10] As a result, the distribution of value added in industry (that is, the shares of value created going to labor costs, profits, and taxes respectively) changed even more in favor of labor, whereas the share of capital (profits) fell to its lowest point since 1954.[11]

As the negative effects of the *plan de refroidissement* became clear, and as the plan coincided with international developments that aggravated the deflationary impact, the government made a complete turnaround. In January 1975, a first *plan de soutien* (support) was announced; then, in September 1975, came the *plan de relance* (reflation), inspired primarily by Jacques Chirac, who was then prime minister. Within a brief period, the policy showed results. Industrial production and economic growth started up again suddenly.[12] The rise of unemployment came to a temporary halt in 1976.[13] Profitability rose, and the number of business bankruptcies declined.[14] Business indebtedness kept on rising, however.[15] Finally, not much was changed in the distribution of value added, and there was only a slight shift from labor to capital.[16]

But the one single factor that doomed the *relance Chirac* more than anything else was the massive foreign trade deficit that it produced. This deficit upset the balance of payments as economic stimulation led to a great increase of imports not paralleled by a similar increase in exports.[17] Chirac seems to have realized as early as January 1976, only a few months after the *plan de relance* was started, that the situation would soon be untenable. Anticipating a deterioration of the situation, which was bound to come and would probably call for a new period of austerity, he urged Giscard to hold early elections for the Parliament, before 1978. Delay, he felt, would spell certain defeat for the Right.[18]

Giscard disagreed with this political analysis, counting on the breakup of the leftist coalition and also on an improvement of the international economic situation. In early 1976 the trade gap widened, and a policy reversal became unavoidable. The split between Giscard and Chirac was over the direction and character of economic policy. Giscard was internationally oriented. He wanted French firms to have multinational dimensions to increase production, competitiveness, and economic efficiency. His policies caused a large number of small businesses to close or declare bankrupcy, which in turn greatly enhanced unemployment and worker unrest. Chirac, on the other hand, came to represent national capital. He was concerned with defending French capitalists from the international market. The conflict between the Gaullists and Giscardists was irreparable. In the summer of 1976, Chirac resigned as prime minister and created a new party, the Reassemblement pour la République (RPR).

Upon Chirac's resignation, the *plan de relance* was scrapped, and Raymond Barre—at the time minister for foreign trade—was appointed prime minister, a charge that he combined at first with that of minister of finance and the economy. "France's best economist," as Giscard called him when he presented him to the nation, was to come up with a plan that would be closer to the inclinations of the president himself. At the time, Barre was not expected to last in office very long—since 1968, prime ministers had succeeded each other rapidly. Barre, however, lasted well beyond the three years that he had assigned himself as necessary for the success of his policy. Altogether he stayed for five years, the second longest term of any prime minister under the Fifth Republic.

I
The Politics of Economic Policy under Giscard

1
The Barre Policy: Rationale and Results

Looking back to the time when he took office, Barre repeatedly stressed that the economic situation in 1976 was approaching disaster. The balance of trade deficit had its counterpart in "inflationary" wage settlements, and the consequences of the 1974 oil crisis had not yet been faced adequately. All this meant that French industry was in no shape to confront the coming years of intensified competition in the world market.

Rationale

In his public statements, Barre stressed inflation, perhaps because he expected it to be a popular theme with the public. But the core of the Barre plan was elsewhere. Its main goal was to strengthen French business firms through increasing their profitability, in particular by holding down wage increases, a policy which would also have the result of holding down imports.[19] The heart of the problem lay in the distribution of value added; here Barre tried to reverse a tendency that had started in the late 1960s. From 1959 to 1968, France's political stability (apart from the Algerian conflict) had its counterpart in the economic sector. The attitude of government toward business and labor during this period remained consistent for a whole decade. The distribution of value added by industry showed that the relative share of the state was declining, while the shares of labor and capital remained roughly stable, or, rather, increased in a parallel fashion.[20]

This stable evolution was interrupted by the May events of 1968. Since that time, redistributional conflicts (under the heading *inégalités sociales*) have occupied a prominent place in French politics, from Jacques Chaban-Delmas's years as prime minister (1969–1972), to the Common Program of the Left (1972), the presidential election of 1974, the goals of the Seventh Plan (1976–1980), and the *plan Barre*. In the Grenelle agreements that settled the industrial conflict after May 1968, wages were increased dramatically. It was widely expected that this would bleed French business white. As a result, the government accorded exceptional assistance to private enterprise (including the devaluation of the franc). These measures went so far that in retrospect the years 1968 and, particularly, 1969 appear as years of extremely high profits; they even lead to an overheating of the economy.[21]

But the effect of the 1968 wage increases was only delayed. The years 1970 and 1971, marked by the socially progressive policies of Premier Chaban-Delmas, saw an important increase in the share of labor at the expense of that of capital. This process was slowed down under his more business-oriented successor, Pierre Messmer, who governed from 1972 until Giscard's election in 1974. The year 1975 brought important changes in this distribution, again to the advantage of labor, and 1976, though reversing the trend, did not bring significant change. Business was far from regaining the ground that it had lost in the preceding year and did not even approach the situation that had prevailed throughout the 1960s.[22]

Barre's reasoning was as follows: If wages could be held constant in real terms, then any increases in productivity would lead to higher profits (or more competitive prices), thus strengthening the financial situation of French firms in a durable way. Stronger and more export-oriented firms would then proceed to make new investments and thus create new employment. (As Barre stressed in 1978, 40 percent of all jobs in industry depend on exports.[23]) In this way the French economic apparatus would be adapted to the changed international division of labor required both by the oil price increases and by French plans to become one of the world's leading industrial powers on a level equal with West Germany. Success of the *plan Barre* would mean that more orders, more profits, and more industrial employment would converge on France—a strategy repeatedly pursued by Germany ever since the end of the nineteenth century.[24] A renewed and triumphant France would then emerge from the trade wars of the 1970s and 1980s.

The measures taken in the implementation of the *plan Barre* can be grouped into three distinct periods. The first period lasted from September 1976 to March 1978. It was marked, as became clear later, by relative moderation, out of concern for the 1978 legislative elections. After the victory of the Right in 1978, the path was cleared for serious action; Barre felt that he was now free to impose his policy without restrictions. Practices that had been established for decades were overthrown in a short time. A third period, marked by a new tightening of policy, began in 1979 in response to the second oil crisis.[25] The presidential election of 1981 does not seem to have had much impact.

The core of the Barre plan was thus to strengthen the financial situation of French business enterprises. In the first period, when prices were still controlled by the government and after a temporary price freeze until December 1976, this was achieved by letting industrial prices rise faster than earlier and by other measures such as accelerated tax write-offs.[26] In addition, Barre promised in his electoral program for the 1978 elections (the *Programme de Blois*) to halt the increase in taxes and social contributions, a promise that he could not or, in any case, did not keep.[27]

Dramatic change came after the 1978 elections. Prices were decontrolled for the first time since the war, and the decree of 1945 on which price controls had been based was abolished altogether.[28] Predictably, prices rose; the stock market went up steeply—in part, undoubtedly, also because of the defeat of the Left—and the indebtedness of French firms receded for the first time in years.[29] Soon afterward, governmental controls of dismissals of the work force for redundancy were greatly relaxed. The government itself showed the way when it took control of the ailing iron and steel industry and imposed a program of extensive layoffs as part of its rescue operation. Similar "shake-outs" followed throughout French industry, despite increased profitability. These developments were further accentuated during the third period; Barre called for an economy where responsible entrepreneurs would make their decisions freely without being burdened, or manipulated, by inefficient state regulations. After 1977, profits clearly recovered.[30]

In Barre's view, the progressive slowdown of wage increases was central to the improvement of the financial situation of French business. Again, the more energetic measures were taken only after 1978. Barre announced then that any business that gave inflationary wage increases (that is, real wage increases exceeding approximately 2 percent) could not count on getting loans, contracts, or protection against imports from the state. Again this broke with a well-established practice, dating back at least to 1945[31] To take the edge off these measures, he promised that the lowest income groups would still be allowed to make further progress, and the government repeatedly acted to increase modestly the purchasing power of the French minimum wage, of old-age pensions, and of family allowances. The idea was also to keep consumption constant because a recession would be damaging to business and might also produce a repetition of the May 1968 events.[32] If necessary, the government would increase expenditures to keep overall consumption constant, an explanation in part for the increasing budget deficits after 1976. Barre stated that he preferred the Swedish social democrats to British Prime Minister Margaret Thatcher or to the economists of the Chicago school, who, in his view, could hardly formulate an effective economic policy on the basis of their principles.[33]

Barre's policy did mean abstention of the state in two areas, however, unemployment and private investment. With regard to unemployment, Barre's attitude was consistently one of benign neglect. He argued that only healthy firms could create viable jobs and listed measures designed to increase business profits as measures to fight unemployment. When in 1977 and 1978 unemployment increased, he said that the situation should not be made to look worse than it really was—after all, he argued, some increase in unemployment was only to be expected after the earlier years of over-employment.[34] Barre claimed, more than a year before the government took over that sector, that a profitable iron and steel industry employing 100 thousand people was much preferable to a sick one employing 150 thousand.[35] A higher growth rate, he admitted, would reduce unemployment but would not lead to more solid business firms. Any such "improvement" was illusory because it was temporary. The only real answer was stronger exports and stronger profits.[36]

Unemployment figures kept creeping up every year

Barre was in office, but the prime minister remained unruffled. The year 1979 brought massive layoffs—most conspicuously in the ailing iron and steel industry, where 22 thousand jobs were eliminated—but several firms such as Saint-Gobain-Pont-à-Mousson, Rhône-Poulenc, or Péchiney-Ugine-Kuhlmann practiced a similar policy, even though they greatly increased their profits during this time period.[37] Barre, however, kept insisting that not all unemployment constituted real hardship; he pointed in particular to the large percentage of unemployed women to say that in the past many of them would not even have looked for employment.[38] In 1979, when the calculations by the National Institute of Statistics and Economic Studies projected the possibility of 2 million unemployed by 1985, and 3 million by 1990, Barre only scoffed and argued that France had "quasi-full employment" and that, in any case, unemployment could only be the byproduct of healthy business firms.[39]

Until the very end, the Giscardiens held the view that stimulation of the economy could only artificially and temporarily absorb unemployment and was bound to lead in turn to an even deeper recession.[40] The only direct measures to help employment consisted of training and employment programs for the young, for whom the state subsidized jobs, and a program that organized (sometimes in a quite repressive way) the return of immigrant workers.[41] In addition, there was a proposal to reduce the retirement age for particularly difficult kinds of work, a proposal to be implemented by negotiation and agreement between the social partners.

According to Barre, private investment, too, was the exclusive province of the business firms. Strong firms would not only be able to make investments, but would also know which investments were best. The main task of the state, therefore, was to improve their financial strength. Again this broke with the well-established tradition in which the French state took an active role in orienting investment—

one of the central tasks of the successive five-year plans. In fact, the lack of investment did cause worry in the ranks of the *Union pour la démocratic françoise* (UDF)—the party that organized the supporters of Giscard.[42] Particularly in 1979, when profits rebounded but did not lead to a significant increase in private investment, this criticism became more intense. Yet Barre insisted that it was up to business to decide on investments; there was no point in having the state encourage investment by specific measures because such a practice could only lead to bad investments. In any case, no such measures were undertaken.[43]

The rate of growth of the national economy, once, like investment, at the core of the five-year plans, was no longer dealt with in a direct way either; the rate would be the result of other variables in the economy. A sound economy, Barre never failed to repeat, was more important than one with high growth rates, though he did note with satisfaction that France's growth rate was still among the highest. It must be added that Barre, and particularly Giscard, were both concerned about the socially disruptive effects of an excessively high growth rate. This preoccupation was more relevant in the early 1970s than toward the end of the decade.[44] It is possible, however, that they thought that slow growth also had its good sides, and certainly Giscard used this argument to appeal for the ecology vote, an element that was far from negligible in France in the 1970s.

Because so much of the success of the *plan Barre* depended on the growth of exports, one might expect to see some measures that would have stimulated them, such as a devalued franc. After all, undervaluation of the national currency had been a crucial element in Germany's success.[45] But in contrast to the policy conducted under President Pompidou, Barre made it clear to industrialists that he would never—never—accept such a measure, and that they had better make their calculations without it. As a result, industrialists felt that they had to recoup their losses or insufficient profit margins by increasing prices in the home market.

In recent years, there has been much discussion of a "political business cycle," in the sense of a stimulation of the economy just before major elections. Some of the actions of the Barre government clearly show sensitivity to electoral considerations, such as the postponement of a real tightening of the *plan Barre* until after March 1978 when the parliamentary elections were out of the way, or the delayed increases of public tariffs in 1981. But, on the whole, Barre adamantly held to his principles: there would be no stimulation of the economy for the sake of Giscard's reelection, whether the president liked it or not.[46] When the 1981 elections came around, the French economy was just reacting to the depth of the recession that resulted from the 1979 oil price increase.[47] As a result, Giscard's last minute plan to reduce unemployment was not particularly credible.[48]

Results

In judging Barre's policy, one has to remember the disruptive events of this period: the oil price increase of 1979, the fluctuation of the dollar, and the rise of export-oriented industries in some Third World countries. Nonetheless, several points emerge quite clearly. As to financial strength of business enterprises, the picture was mixed.[49] There was considerable improvement of profitability from 1977 to 1979. (After the catastrophic year 1975, the *plan de relance* of 1976 brought a relatively good year.) But in 1980, when the effect of the second oil crisis came to be felt, there was renewed deterioration. In other areas, furthermore, there was little or no improvement. Thus indebtedness kept on rising, and taxes and social contribution also continued their upward trend. The rise in social contributions was felt as a particular hardship by business; it reflected the increasing unemployment because the French unemployment insurance system relies heavily on employers' contributions. Business bankruptcies also increased further above the level of the 1975 deflation and were rising again by 1980.[50] The continued financial vulnerability of business, combined with the absence of any prospect for expansion given Barre's policy, helps explain the investment behavior depicted by Jacky Fayolle in November 1980, which showed that from 1960 to 1970 both the investment rate and the financing of investments from retained earnings (*autofinancement*) were relatively high.[51] In 1971, the investment rate began to fall, and so, for some time, did *autofinancement*. From 1976 onward, however, the share of investments financed from retained earnings increased considerably. Yet at the same time, the investment rate itself continued its long-term decline from 1970—except for a brief reversal in 1976, due to the *relance Chirac*. French business had become very cautious about investing. The investment gap that had opened in the early 1970s remained wide, even if there were modest signs of improvements toward the end of the 1970s.[52]

The government could not claim particular success with inflation; during Barre's tenure, inflation rates in France remained consistently above that of a reference group of Western industrial countries. It was unavoidable that sooner or later this would have an impact on the franc's relation to other currencies. Real wages, despite the spartan rhetoric of the government, in fact progressed at a higher rate in France than in the European Community, the United States, or Japan.[53] There was, however, a marked slowdown as the Barre years wore on.[54] The share of personnel costs in the distribution of value added seemed more or less stabilized.[55]

The balance of trade showed improvement in 1977 and 1978, and in 1979 and 1980 the deficit at least seemed not too large when compared to the disastrous results of 1976.

But the cost of this policy was also clear. Imports were held down by limiting growth; there was a clear downward trend in the rate of growth of the gross domestic product. True, in comparative terms the French performance was not all that bad for the years 1974-1981. Among the major industrial countries, only Japan had a higher growth rate during this period. But after 1978, France began to fall behind, in particular behind West Germany, which also had a considerably lower unemployment rate.[56] To leaders preoccupied with French-German economic rivalry, Barre's performance fell scandalously short of long-held French ambitions.

2
The Political Environment: The Right

Whatever the intrinsic value of Barre's policy, the fact remains that it came to be disapproved, soon after its inception, by three of the four major—and, in the 1978 elections, roughly equal—political parties.[57] In addition, there were some mild reservations even in the ranks of the UDF, Barre's own party, concerning mostly the question of national solidarity in times of economic hardship. Too much of the burden, so went the reservations, was carried by the unemployed and by wage earners; something had to be done to alleviate their condition such as a solidarity tax on the very wealthy or on inheritances to finance public works, retraining, and relief.[58]

The attitude of the RPR (the Gaullists, renamed by Jacques Chirac when he reorganized them in late 1976) was quite different. It evolved from support for Barre's policy in the first year, to open criticism before the 1978 elections, and, finally, to increasingly bitter, even vicious attacks. True, not all Gaullists participated in this; many of them thought that the first duty of the party was to support the action of the government, even if they did not agree with it in important respects. In addition, some Gaullist leaders served in the Barre government as ministers. They were not the only ones, though, to support openly its economic policy.[59] As a result, there was no coherent Gaullist line, especially as Chirac himself changed his own position considerably over the years. In addition, there was a practical problem: What could be done to change Barre's policy? Some Gaullists went so far as to propose voting a censure motion against the government. But in the end, the party shrank from an act most members must have perceived as akin to regicide.[60]

Given the economic philosophy of Barre and Giscard, a conflict with the Gaullists was unavoidable sooner or later. One of the principles of de Gaulle (and of Gaullism after him) was that the political goals of the state would be set down first; the state would then intervene in the economy in such a way as to achieve the desired results. Prominent among the goals of the state were national greatness, national cohesion, and active modernization. For Gaullists, these notions implied political action on investments, employment, wages, and economic growth. After the withdrawal of the general from public affairs, Gaullist rhetoric became more subdued, but a strong interventionist practice remained.

It is true that some Gaullists began to see excessive state involvement as a cause of economic inefficiency.[61] Nonetheless, the old reflexes and practices persisted among most of the leaders of the movement, in particular Chirac. The *plan de relance* of 1975–1976 had been his brainchild, and, under his leadership, the RPR made it increasingly clear that if only the Gaullists had more power, they would never accept that the nation be turned over to, or martyrized by, market forces.[62] They would not stand by as France suffered internationally, with investments and growth rate falling (a setback for national greatness) and unemployment rising (endangering national cohesion and thus power). Unsuccessfully they pressed again and again for a more active economic policy and criticized not only the government's programs (consisting mostly of inaction, in their view) but also its soothing rhetoric. Barre and Giscard, the Gaullists said, were lulling the country into a false optimism with their statements that things were not really all that bad and would in any case improve before long. The Gaullists wanted to awaken the country. They wanted to mobilize, to galvanize France by stirring appeals to action, sacrifice, and solidarity.[63]

Chirac's resignation in 1976 had taken place against a background of differences with Giscard regarding both economic strategy and political analysis. At first, Chirac remained quiet, and the Gaullists supported Barre's policy; then they became more critical with the *plan Barre bis* in the fall of 1977. Criticism mounted with the approach of the 1978 elections. Forceful proposals were advanced in favor of another *relance,* or massive reflation, through a promotion of both investment and employment by the state and big industry.[64] The Keynesian nature of this strategy was made even clearer by a proposal calling for a new Marshall Plan, one that would use the surpluses of Arab oil producers to finance the development needs of African countries, which in turn would result in an increase in the demand for industrial goods produced and exported by Western Europe.[65] Inflation would be held down by improving productivity through lower unit costs. (French industry was running below capacity.) By the fall of 1979, however, the idea of a reflation (*relance globale*) was abandoned in favor of a "new growth" (*nouvelle croissance*) based on a massive investment campaign.[66] These investments were to prepare France for the coming years of international economic warfare; they would develop exports, reconquer domestic markets for French industry, increase the growth rate, and, in due course, create new jobs.

One main point over which Gaullists and Barre disagreed most strongly was the role of the state in private investment. Barre left the matter up to the entrepreneurs, arguing that intervention by the state could only distort economic efficiency. Such a proposition was quite unacceptable to Gaullists: to them the duty of the state is to guide investment. They claimed that liberal capitalism has simply proven inefficient. The nation pays for what business cannot do, or does not do correctly and swiftly enough.[67] Chirac resorted to strong language: he compared business investments to armaments. In 1979, he declared that under the conditions of economic warfare in which France found itself, one could of course rearm (read: invest) slowly—as France had done in 1938—while others rearmed rapidly; but if France continued down this road, it was headed for another *débâcle* along the lines of 1940.[68]

These appeals for vigorous action by the state on the investment front to restructure French industry and agriculture were repeated with the *rapport Méo* in the fall of 1979. This report became for some time the centerpiece of Gaullist thinking about the economy.[69] Journalists noted, however, that the Gaullists had little to say about how these investments would be financed, because at the same time they disapproved of Barre's budget deficit, causing a minor political crisis at the end of 1979.[70]

Chirac made an effort to answer those questions in an interview with *Le Monde* in April 1980.[71] The necessary funds (10-15 billion francs for investment alone, public and private) would be obtained, he argued, by reducing state expenditures on personnel, on unemployment compensation—by reducing unemployment from 1.5 million to 500 thousand—an exceptional tax on wealth, and other measures. He was also more specific about where the investments should go. Overall, his policy in all areas called for an additional expenditure of 30 billion francs per year (6 percent of the national budget). But the possibility of raising such funds without increasing the budget deficit or aggravating inflation was again received with skepticism.

To Gaullists, private business has a public function; this is what justifies intervention. Business may need to be encouraged, even prodded, to make the right investments. It may also need to be helped and protected. Even Michel Debré, who outdid all other Gaullists in his appeals to sacrifice in what he saw as one of the great national crises in French history, rejected what he termed Barre's unfair policy of letting the weaker firms go bankrupt.[72] Debré, as well as Chirac, proposed resorting to protective measures to save French industries endangered by imports.[73]

Employment, like investment, cannot be left to market forces in the Gaullist view. Nor do Gaullists like to pit wages against profits, or employment against investment, as Barre was doing. *Propositions pour la France,* the RPR's program for the 1978 elections, stated that unemployment is morally and socially unacceptable and economically unjustifiable, no matter what experts might say. The program also proposed an aggressive strategy of job creation.[74] Perhaps in response to the oil price increases of 1979, later statements, starting with the *rapport Méo,* stressed investment-led growth and left out consumption-led growth altogether. But even then Gaullists were persuaded that some progress in wages was necessary for the sake of national unity. As Jean Méo, Chirac's economic adviser, put it, "one could not lead the country from tunnel to tunnel"—to do so was to invite a social explosion along the lines of May 1968.[75] But the most important proposal for wage earners, apart from the promise to reduce unemployment, was the rediscovery of de Gaulle's theory of *participation* after years of oblivion. Chirac talked about it with fervor and enthusiasm. Participation was the main avenue of social progress, all the more so since real wage increases had become more difficult.[76] However, neither the Giscardiens nor the employers, not to speak of the unions or the parties of the Left, thought much of that idea.

Along with investment and employment, a high rate of economic growth is also, in the minds of the Gaullists, to be promoted by political intervention. Barre played down its importance, would set no targets, and seemed happy with modest percentages. It is true that at one point Chirac seemed to have espoused Giscard's views on the subject, that is that high growth rates were not only unrealistic, but also socially disruptive.[77] But *Propositions pour la France* mentioned a 5 to 6 percent real growth rate as an urgent national goal, and Chirac soon made bitter attacks on Giscard's idea of a *croissance douce* ("gentle growth"); it was gentle, he said, only for the rich.[78] Jean Méo in 1979 proposed a target of 5 percent, double the growth rate at the time, and Chirac argued that in any case the French growth rate must be higher than that of France's main trading partners.[79]

Not all the Gaullists shared the critical attitude of their party leader; many remained loyal to the government. There were other confusing elements, and Chirac changed his strategy repeatedly. Not only did he shift from reflation (*relance globale*) to investment and export-led growth, discovering small and medium-sized business in the process, Chirac added to the confusion by a surprising shift just before the elections. After his statements of early 1980 in which he had called for a spending program of 30 billion francs and also praised President Jimmy Carter for his job-creation initiatives, he now discovered supply-side economics. In February 1981, Chirac announced that as president he would cut back the budget by the very same figure of 30 billion francs —and in the process liberate business initiative from excessive taxes and choking state regulations. He even seemed to repudiate his proposal of an exceptional tax on wealth. It was in blatant contrast to what he had said and (in 1975–1976) had done.

To compound the confusion, the Gaullists went into the 1981 election not with one candidate but with three. A fourth candidate, Michel Jobert, was unable to secure the necessary number of signatures endorsing his candidacy. Before

Chirac, Michel Debré had already announed his candidacy; he was followed by Marie-France Garaud, who, under Pompidou, and afterward, along with Pierre Juillet, had long played the role of *éminence grise* of Gaullist leaders. This was the state of affairs of Barre's main coalition partner on the eve of the 1981 election.

3

The Political Environment: The Left

In the first decade of the Fifth Republic, the Left was in disarray, and its electoral performance fell to unprecedented lows.[80] But the early 1970s saw the rebirth of the Socialist Party, and, under the leadership of François Mitterand, the emergence of a strategy based on the unity of the Left—on cooperation between Socialists and the Communist Party (PCF). This strategy was drawn from experiences that showed that a "third force" or centrist strategy was condemned to fail under the institutions of the Fifth Republic.[81] In 1972 this led to the signature of the *Programme Commun de la Gauche* (the Common Program of the Left) by the two main parties of the Left, and later also by the *Radicaux de Gauche*, a small centrist party. This program was pervaded by the spirit of the long postwar boom, which was then in its last years. It called for a record growth rate, exceeding even that of the Pompidou years, a massive program of redistribution in favor of wage earners and households through such steps as increases in wages, allocations and public services, and a limited number of specified nationalizations. The program was in many respects close to the Communist position on economic issues, as expressed in 1968 in the *Manifeste de Champigny*.[82] In 1972, however, the Marxist wing of the Socialist Party—the Centre d'études de recherches et déducation socialistes (the CERES)—was very influential; its leader, Jean-Pierre Chevènement, was one of the negotiators of the program and had represented the Socialists in the nationalization negotiations.[83]

The Left made considerable progress at the 1973 elections for which the program had been drawn up, and 1974 saw the high point of leftist unity—but also its decline. In the premature presidential elections that followed Pompidou's death, Mitterrand ran as the only candidate of the two big parties of the Left and came very close to the score achieved by Giscard. He did not base his campaign on the Common Program, however, though he never disavowed it, but on more modest—and probably more rigorous—proposals, incorporating the advice of Jacques Attali and Michel Rocard. The Communists remained loyal throughout the campaign, but distrust began to increase with the *Assises du socialisme* in the fall of 1974. This conference brought new elements into the Socialist Party, elements that were mainly committed to the idea of *autogestion* (or self-management) socialism and were openly critical of the Common Program's emphasis on growth and redistribution, while leaving intact the hierarchies of power, which they blamed for the distorted priorities of the economy, and the general direction of development.[84]

Nonetheless the program remained the basic reference text of the Left for several more years, although Mitterrand did not refrain from formulating more specific plans to deal with the economic situation, responding to changing circumstances. The government (even Chirac's) was criticized for its austerity and blamed for the rise in unemployment that the Socialists said would automatically follow.[85] When Barre became prime minister, the Socialists argued that no policy could improve economic conditions in France unless it increased consumption. Even if firms were given tax breaks as incentives to invest, Socialists argued, they would not make any investments unless they could expect to sell their product, something that required strong domestic markets. Because the austerity policies of the government were depressing those markets, they placed the French economy in a vicious circle.[86] Already in 1975 the Socialists proposed the creation of jobs in the public sector, which they said was understaffed. This plan—and a new economic boom—could progressively absorb unemployment.

At first, many Socialists saw in the *plan Barre* nothing but a maneuver for the upcoming 1978 elections. Barre, they predicted, would first slow down the economy and thus hold down inflation. This would be followed by a program of economic stimulation just in time for the March 1978 elections.[87] Yet during the same time the Socialists also worked to enhance the credibility of their own proposals; in particular, they stressed their commitment to an internationally open market economy, despite the nationalizations to which they continued to adhere.[88] In their efforts they received unexpected help from the Communists—though that help was bought initially at a very high political price.

The Communists insisted that the Common Program be updated in preparation for the 1978 elections. Mitterrand disliked the idea, since he expected to be outbid by Communist proposals for high increases of wages and allocations, high public service spending, and the like, proposals that were likely to be made without too much concern for economic realism and might, in the most extreme case, prepare the way for a closed command economy. (A leftist government might find itself nationalizing the firms driven into bankruptcy by excessive costs and resorting to protectionist measures to stave off collapse.) During the negotiations between the two parties, there was considerable discussion of the level at which the new minimum wage was to be set in the event of a leftist victory. The Socialists finally gave in reluctantly after considerable opposition, especially from Michel Rocard.[89])

The main conflict, however, centered on the question of nationalizations. The Socialists, led in these negotiations by Rocard, wanted to stick to the list of firms laid down in the Common Program. The Communists, on the other hand, wanted to add all the hundreds of subsidiaries of those firms. Rocard rejected this proposal with the argument that to do so was both unnecessary and wasteful: It would require the government to expropriate minority capital that was powerless anyhow. Even without such a measure the control of the parent firm meant a majority participation in the subsidiary —and therefore brought effective control.[90] Clearly, what the Communists rejected was the idea that the nationalized firms would remain subject to the laws of the market. In any case, it was over the issue of nationalizations that the break between the Socialists and Communists occurred in the fall of 1977, a break that sealed the fate of the Left in the 1978 elections.

Now the mood in the Socialist Party changed. For years this mood had been optimistic, based on the assumption that the Left would come to power soon. In fact, the Left achieved a clear majority of votes at the regional elections in 1976 and the municipal elections of 1977. But the break of 1977, and the subsequent defeat in 1978, threw the Socialist Party into a crisis of demoralization, recriminations, and declining militancy. Rocard and Pierre Mauroy, who, after Mitterrand, had been the most important leaders in the party, now moved away from him. This evolution was consecrated at the party congress in Metz, in the spring of 1979, at which their two currents formed the new "internal opposition."[91] Many of the high civil servants who had jumped on the bandwagon when the party seemed to be headed for victory dropped out again, and the morale as well as the number of militants declined.[92] There seemed to be no end to internal disagreements, even though the party was at the same time being attacked from the outside by the Communists, who blamed it for the break of 1977. This critique found an echo inside the party with the leaders of the CERES, Mitterrand's new allies, who now attacked Rocard for the "economic rigor" that brought Rocard positive responses even from the world of business.[93]

It was in this atmosphere that Mitterrand developed his economic program of June 1979, which, at the time, met with relatively little public response. The program apparently was not influenced by Rocard, Mauroy, or even Chevènement.[94] In many ways it was similar to the earlier programs, but it also brought some innovations. Economic stimulation via consumption still played an important role in it, but, like the Gaullist program that was to be submitted a few months later, Mitterrand's program placed greater emphasis than before on investments, more than in the adapted version of the Common Program submitted by the Socialists in January 1978. There were also proposals to reduce French dependence on international trade, to eliminate generalized price controls and restrict them to those areas where competition was not effective, and to proceed with greater caution in the area of job creation. The program, however, still insisted on the 35 hour week without reduction in wages as well as reduced age limits for retirement (60 years for men, 55 for women). Reduction of inequalities was still stressed, but no specific figures were given either for the minimum wage or for financing the program in general. *Autogestion* was not mentioned, but many of the ecology themes were incorporated.

The program proposed a qualitatively different form of economic development that was to be less resource-intensive and oriented toward better consumption and more durable goods rather than toward maximizing consumption. It promised a life in which happiness, security, and the environment would not be sacrificed to the economic calculus. The return to full employment was part of the program, but, here again, no time schedule or specific figures were given except for the creation of jobs in the public sector. Finally, three firms were added to the nationalization list.[95]

The reaction of leading journalists was similar to that given the Gaullist program a few months later: Would it be possible to finance all this? Would it be possible to hold down inflation simultaneously? In addition, were the goals for reduced international trade and energy consumption realistic? But even *Les Echos,* the French counterpart to the *Wall Street Journal,* wrote that the program appeared "more realistic," even if it still contained quite a few "dreams."[96]

The internal divisions within the party lasted through a good part of 1980 as seen in internal party discussions over the *Project socialiste,* early in the year and again later with the approach of the presidential elections.[97] Rocard wanted to be the party's candidate and did extremely well in pre-electoral polls, considerably better than Mitterrand.[98] He was prepared to yield to Mitterrand, however, but when, by October, Mitterrand still had not declared his intentions, Rocard announced his own candidacy, withdrawing three weeks later when Mitterrand entered the race.[99]

All this was a far cry from the unity preceding the 1974 presidential elections, especially as the Communists now insisted on running their own candidate. But Rocard maintained party discipline and promised to work hard for Mitterrand's election. As for the Communists, the Socialists had learned since 1977 to deal more effectively with the Communist Party's tactics that were designed to insure the defeat of the Left altogether rather than have the Communist Party lose votes. After some hesitation, Mitterrand, who insisted on leftist unity, appealed to Communist voters and sympathizers over the heads of the Communist Party, a method that was highly successful in 1981.[100] What were the main assets of Socialist economic proposals in 1981? First, the party was well prepared on all the important issues and did not have to come up with last-minute ideas. It proposed to take energetic action to deal with unemployment. The Socialists also made effective use of the calculations of the National Institute of Statistics and Economic Studies that projected a further rise in unemployment; Giscard and Barre had little to counter that. Whereas in 1974 the Socialists had been handicapped by the perceptions that Giscard was more likely than Mitterrand to "assure the development of the economy," this image changed during the following years.[101] At the end of the 1970s, the Socialist commitment to a successful and internationally open market economy was hardly in doubt, if only because of the clarifying conflicts with the Communists over that issue.

Rightist claims that a victory for Mitterrand would be tantamount to the installment of a closed command economy could hardly sound plausible in 1981.[102] The economic strategies of the Socialists were taken quite seriously by part of the business press.[103] Individual measures such as the 35-hour week were evaluated by the Planning Commission and found not only viable but even beneficial for employment and for investment and would lead only to a minor increase in state debt.[104] Nationalizations may have lost their appeal in a country such as Britain, but in France they have a good record and they are quite popular.[105] France has a very successful public sector, one of the largest in Western Europe and one that includes many of the major banks and companies such as Renault and Aérospatiale.[106] In general, the Socialists seemed to be in touch with economic realities. By 1977, the Socialist Party was the largest political party in France and had become the party whose electoral support most resembled the sociological characteristics of the electorate as a whole. The Socialists had also begun to impede on the Communists' traditional working-class electoral base. In addition, they seemed to be in better contact than most other parties with the new social movements of the 1970s, especially ecology, antinuclear, and feminist movements. Finally, the Socialists were greatly helped by Gaullist attacks on Barre and Giscard. Many critiques and proposals were common to the Socialists and the Gaullists. Shortly before the election, an economic adviser to Mitterrand recognized the similarity between the Gaullist strategy in 1975-1976 and that of the Socialists in the stimulation of demand, except that the Gaullists did not—and were not prepared to —take the same structural measures that would have modified the conditions of supply.[107] With regard to economic proposals, the Socialists and, most of the time, the Gaullists were closest to that center from which Giscard hoped to rule the nation. Barre on the other hand was at one extreme with his "liberalism," which was neatly mirrored by the command-economy approach of the Communists.

The evolution of the Communist Party is in striking contrast to that of the Socialist Party. In the late 1960s and early 1970s, the PCF had been the stronger party of the Left; from then on it declined, not necessarily in absolute, but at least in relative, terms as compared to the Socialists.[108] To the Communist leadership, relative weight was just as important, as the leadership of the Left was at stake. Mitterrand never made any bones about his intentions to create a "new equilibrium" on the Left, one more favorable to the Socialists. As a result, as early as 1972, Georges Marchais, the leader of the Communist Party, was suspicious of him: could Mitterrand be trusted to practice something other than a social democratic policy if he were to come to power? For this reason, particular emphasis was placed on the Common Program, which the Communists had strongly influenced; it would bind the Socialists publicly. Furthermore, the militant basis of the Communist Party was several times stronger than that of the Socialist Party, providing an additional guaranty.[109]

In the 1974 elections, however, the Communists gave Mitterrand free rein, while also giving full support to his candidacy. Misgivings arose in autumn 1974 with the *Assises du socialisme,* which indicated not only that the Socialist Party was moving away from the Common Program but also that it was setting out to obtain a working class base through the Confédération française démocratique du travail (CFDT), France's second largest labor union, whose leaders were prominent in the *Assises.* This would challenge the PCF on its home turf.[110] Fears about Socialist emancipation were reinforced by the latter's emphatic commitments to a market economy in 1976 and also by the realization that electoral cooperation benefited primarily the Socialists.

The paradoxical result was that even as the PCF continued its own liberalization, its attitude toward the Socialist Party became more and more rigid. By 1981, the resulting strains effectively put an end to internal PCF liberalization. At all costs the Socialists had to be reined in by the Common Program, which was now given an even stricter interpretation. This explains the break of 1977 during the updating negotiations, which formally occurred over the issue of the subsidiaries of the companies that were to be nationalized.[111] The Socialists were accused of accepting the "logic of profit." Under these circumstances, the PCF leadership decided that it was better to lose an election rather than help a Socialist Party that, once in power, would "continue the policy of big capital."[112]

Since that time, with a brief lull in 1979, the Communists have launched continuous attacks on the Socialists. In March 1980, *L'Humanité,* the party's daily, declared that there was no real difference between the big industrialists,

Barre, or even Mitterrand.[113] Events in Afghanistan and Poland fueled the conflict. In the autumn of 1980, the Communists refused the long-established practice of cooperation with the Socialists in the senatorial elections.[114] Their first priority became the reassertion of their own identity against an increasingly hegemonic Socialist Party.

Once the ambiguous compromise of the Common Program was abandoned, the economic views of the Communist Party also underwent a clarification. The analysis of the economic crisis was generally in the traditional mold: it was all due to the overaccumulation of capital by national and international monopolies, causing in turn the overexploitation of the working class.[115] The oil crisis only served as an alibi for the capitalist offensive against the working class conducted by the Barre government. Both Giscard and Barre were acting hand-in-glove with the designs of international capital to dismantle French industry in the search for higher profit rates elsewhere.[116]

If there was an innovation, the PCF placed greater emphasis on international capital rather than on state monopoly capitalism. The answer to the crisis—and here the French Communist Party disagreed with its Italian counterpart under Enrico Berlinguer—was not an economic policy of fairly shared austerity, but a wholesale rejection of the logic of profit, coupled with economic nationalism. It was the capitalist concern with profits that led to shutdowns and layoffs. This criterion needed to be replaced with the new one of "social profitability" that would lead to the greater satisfaction of needs and thus to higher output.[117]

The issue of nationalizations was crucial because the Communist approach of state control was quite different from that of the Socialists. If the Socialists were satisfied with a controlling interest in the subsidiaries, it was because they were prepared to accept the discipline of the market for all firms. To the Communists, this meant accepting the "logic of profit." The conflict was replayed in the same terms over the issue of the steel industry. Again the Socialists, despite their opposition to Barre's handling of the problem, were quite prepared to accept the sanction of the market, while the Communists refused it, proposing nationalization, expansion of production, and an end to all layoffs.[118]

One of the criticisms of the Common Program had long been that it would make protectionism unavoidable and thus lead to a weakening of France's international position as well as a decline in the standard of living. While there was always ambiguity on this point, the Communists stepped up their nationalist rhetoric during the late 1970s.[119] The Communists tried to exploit residual anti-German feelings and racial prejudice in their campaigns against immigrant workers. In 1981 Marchais said that, "in certain cases," it could be necessary to protect French industry and agriculture and perhaps keep out foreign products. But he did not discuss the problem of possible foreign retaliation.[120]

Thus the two parties of the Left had moved apart during the Barre era. Still, there were considerable similarities: the Communists also proposed redistribution of income (though on a much larger scale than the Socialists) and advocated full employment policies. They supported the 35-hour week, earlier retirement, nationalizations, and greatly improved public services and investments. On their side, the Socialists maintained the slogan of a "break with capitalism." Unlike Chirac, Marchais announced in advance whom he would support in the second round of the 1981 presidential election. Despite his own candidacy, he would recommend a vote for François Mitterrand.[121]

4

Business and Labor

The mid-1970s were a difficult time for many French employers. There were immediate economic reasons: interest rates had been rising for some time, taking up an increasing share of the return on capital; wages also rose, and in 1974 dismissals had become more difficult. Concurrently, financing of investments from retained earnings fell, indebtedness increased, and investment stagnated, particularly in large firms.[122]

The political evolution also added to the demoralization: the Left was showing considerable strength in polls and elections, and in the autumn of 1976, a survey conducted by the monthly *L'Expansion* showed that employers expected that the Left would win the 1978 legislative elections by a ratio of 3:1.[123] That possibility was viewed with distress by most private sector employers, who seemed to think that the Common Program was committed not only to redistribution but would, in the words of the Conseil National du Patronat Français (CNPF, the French Employers' Association), put an end to free enterprise and make France the home of collectivism. Mitterrand and many Socialists might not approve of that, but they would inevitably be dominated by the Communists and their methods.[124] Not surprisingly, many employers participated actively in the propaganda battle against the Left. Some firms that were targets for nationalization entered into agreements with foreign businesses to make that process more difficult, if not impossible. Also, some capital flight occurred just before the elections. On the whole, demoralization was widespread.[125]

But with the breakup of leftist unity in the fall of 1977, demoralization changed camp. Barre's policy was now supported and praised. At the same time, the CNPF came forward with interpretations and proposals that showed that in some ways its approach differed from that of the government. Like Barre, this organization stressed the need to strengthen private enterprise financially and advocated complete decontrol of prices, the amortization of assets by calculating them at their real value, and measures to encourage stock ownership. It urged a reduction of fiscal and social charges and similar measures. The CNPF also joined the prime minister in advocating a deflationary cure and the need to hold down wage increases in particular. The organization viewed such a policy as a temporary expedient, however, believing that an austerity that lasted too long was bound to weaken the economy.

Consequently, as early as October 1976 the CNPF expressed worry about the anticipated decline in demand and asked for prompt supportive measures within a few months. Without these, it warned, there would have to be another *plan Barre* against unemployment by September 1977.[126] France needed a high growth rate to solve her social problems, which required a high rate of investment.[127] In the eyes of the CNPF, investment had fallen behind for two reasons: low demand and the fragile situation of many French business firms.[128]

Early in 1977, Jacques Ferry, one of the leaders of the

CNPF, argued in his yearly report that the medicine of Barre should not last longer than one year, after which it should be possible to return to growth. He also called for a policy favorable to industry, one that would be more energetic than the one practiced by the government. This would require financially strong French enterprises, to be sure, but it also required a framework set up by the state. The elements of such a framework were a five-year plan ("the affirmation of an autonomous will to promote... a certain rate of growth") and a solid government doctrine regarding international trade.[129] Totally free trade, Ferry argued, was unacceptable and tantamount to a surrender to U.S. hegemony. Too many countries took advantage of such a state of affairs to practice their own kind of dumping on the French market through such measures as undervalued currencies and low wages. This was leading to untenable situations in such sectors as textiles, steel, and shipbuilding. Ferry believed it was important for the government to react promptly whenever a whole sector of the French economy was threatened.

Thus, the CNPF was asking openly for a more active role by the state, while distinguishing this from interventionism or the *dirigisme* to be expected from the Left. Barre did not really live up to these expectations, however. He believed too much in international competition and preferred to rely on measures designed to strengthen French business at the level of the individual firm without discriminating between different sectors.

The CNPF continued to call for a higher rate of growth in the early years of the *plan Barre*. This was the only way to resolve the problem of unemployment, especially as the system of unemployment compensation was weighing too heavily on the firms and thus stood in need of revision.[130] France could not long continue with a growth rate of only 3 or 3.5 percent per year. The key to progress in this area was investment and an energetic industrial policy on the part of the state, which would outline the "great options" and "protect . . . without becoming protectionist."[131] In October 1979, the daily *Les Echos,* close to the business world, proposed stimulating investment with an injection of 25 billion francs. This, it argued, was the logical continuation of the *plan Barre,* the first part of which was now "successfully completed" by deflation and the return of financial health among French firms. The 25 billion would stimulate initiative and awaken those energies that Barre's policy had necessarily discouraged in the past.[132] This proposal coincided with the Gaullist's *rapport Méo,* and the Socialists had also been stressing investments in their earlier June 1979 proposals.

But the accommodation between the partners of the presidential coalition, clearly hoped for in business circles, did not take place.[133] Instead, Barre only tightened his policy even further, and André Giraud, the French minister of industry, stressed that it was not up to the state to choose those industrial sectors that should undergo the strongest expansion. The state's role, he argued, was to place each enterprise in a position that would allow it to be a winner in the international competition.[134] It is true that a CNPF spokesman supported this approach. Recent experience had shown, he argued, that the grand macroeconomic strategies were ill-adapted to a time of crisis, whereas individual business firms could react much more quickly.[135] In fact, some business circles criticized the government for not going far enough in its support of private enterprise, particularly with measures improving the financial situation of business firms.[136]

Overall, in business circles as in the governmental majority there was no clear consensus on a fully open economy or the conditions of success.[137] These differences in approach were reflected in different electoral attitudes in 1981. Big business was on the whole favorable to Giscard, but small and medium-sized businesses were far more likely to favor

Chirac. Only a narrow majority of the big employers thought well of Giscard's economic policy by 1980; most of the smaller ones would have preferred something else.[138]

An absence of unity on the employer side was reflected in the labor unions; they also could not agree on the economic situation. This should not be a surprise given the division of the French labor movement. Of the three large industrial unions, the smallest, the Force ouvrière, is openly reformist and apolitical; the strongest, the Confédération générale du travail (CGT) is for all practical purposes Communist and an extension of the French Communist Party with which it shares some of the top leaders; and the third, the CFDT, is oriented toward *autogestion* socialism, open toward the new social movements of the 1970s, and, despite its closeness with the Socialist Party since the *Assises du socialisme* in 1974, quite jealous of its political independence.

The CGT, like the Communist Party, had long been relegated to the ghetto; it emerged from there in the mid-1960s. An important step in this process was an agreement with the CFDT according to which the two unions were to coordinate their action, corresponding to developments at the level of the political parties of the Left.[139] After a period in which the unions' fortunes were better than those of the political parties closest to them (1968-1972), the coordination with those parties was greatest from 1973 to the end of 1977.[140] In 1974 both unions supported the candidacy of Mitterrand, and at one point their leaders even shared a podium with the candidate of the United Left.[141] During this period, the two unions placed all their hopes for a radical transformation of society on an election that would bring the Left to power. This led to the neglect of the more traditional trade union activities. Neither the *plan Barre* nor the economic crisis were taken very seriously at first, because the 1978 elections were to put an end to all this anyhow.[142] The shock was all the greater in September 1977, when the negotiations on the revision of the Common Program broke down. As in the case of the parties of the Left, the optimistic mood of the leadership in the two revolutionary unions now gave way to a phase of demoralization, recrimination, and a greater divergence in their thinking. In addition, they both developed their autonomy vis-à-vis the political parties they were close to. This was particularly true of the CFDT. As early as January 1978, it prepared for the possibility of a defeat by its *recentrage* (reorientation). The leadership announced that it had gone too far in subordinating the union's strategy to events in party and electoral politics—such a strategy had left little initiative to the union and its members and thus had encouraged passivity. It was time to remember that society was not changed by elections alone. The struggle was a much broader one, and unions had an independent role to play. Edmond Maire, the leader of the CFDT, had said that much in this earlier critique of the Common Program. The CFDT now emphasized the struggle against unemployment, the need to increase the lowest incomes despite the crisis, the improvement of working conditions, and the new concerns such as the critique of the rapid development of nuclear power and of "productivism" generally. By the end of 1978, the CGT, in turn, discovered the need for more trade unionist practices.[143]

With regard to the economic crisis that had settled on much of the Western world, the outlook of the unions diverged very sharply. The Force ouvrière argued for accepting the necessity of industrial adaptation, even though its leader, André Bergeron, was to criticize the government later for letting unemployment rise to such high levels.[144] The CFDT and the CGT both criticized Barre in much stronger terms. The CFDT thought the situation serious; it did not simply argue for the stimulation of consumption and protectionism but took a more selective approach, recognizing the need for industrial restructuring to remain competitive but stressing the possibility of developing French industries in areas where imports were very high.[145] At the same time, the CFDT argued that the cost of adaptation should be distributed differently across the population. The need to remain competitive in the world economy did not mean that social progress had to come to a halt; it merely meant that further improvements required coordination with the other countries of the European Community.[146]

The approach of the CGT was different and followed that of the Communist Party: the crisis was merely a crisis of capitalism and perhaps just a pretext under which advantages obtained by the working class in the past were to be undermined or forcibly taken back. All that was needed, the CGT claimed, was a massive stimulation of consumption and energetic measures to protect the French economy against the disruptions coming from abroad in a framework that would generally reject the capitalist logic of profit. The way to achieve progress was to put pressure on the government and the capitalists. Thus the CGT sponsored a series of mass demonstrations to show the public the massive discontent among French workers. Such actions, the union proclaimed, would soon put an end to the capitalist offensive.[147]

These mass demonstrations, however, which the CFDT resisted, were never quite as massive as the CGT leadership had hoped. The economic crisis, reinforced no doubt by political defeat, had taken its toll on the revolutionary unions, particularly the CGT, but to a lesser extent also on the CFDT. (Only the reformist Force ouvrière seemed to attract a greater audience, at the expense of the two other unions.) The decline started, surprisingly, in the heyday of leftist unity, in 1974 and 1975. Union membership in some probably quite typical firms fell as much as 50 percent over a period of five years. The voting strength of the CGT in professional elections actually declined.[148] Also declining was the number of work days lost to strikes, despite a rebound in 1979, a year in which the number of strikes was high throughout the Western world.[149]

Militancy was generally on the decline. Most of the workers were worried about their jobs and seemed more open to employers' arguments. Furthermore, the unions were unable to secure new advantages as long as the recession lasted. The employers did their best to accelerate this movement. They developed a conscious strategy of cutting down the unions by setting up mechanisms that bypassed the unions to demonstrate their futility. Despite the resistance of the unions, that approach seemed to be quite successful.[150]

Finally, organized labor in France was increasingly handicapped by the struggle between the two main unions. The CGT mirrored the PCF in its attacks on the Socialists and on the CFDT, which it accused of shifting to the Right. As with the great parties of the Left, international events (in particular in Afghanistan and Poland) led to increased tensions. Although there was no definite break, there was little cooperation.

The approaching elections of 1981 did nothing to bridge the gap—perhaps because the unions did not expect the Left to win or did not want to tie their fortunes once more to a candidate whose success was uncertain. Besides, there was no common candidate of the Left in the first round, and the CGT became an electoral machine for Marchais, the Communist candidate. This caused considerable tension within the union. Even after the first round of elections, the CGT was less than enthusiastic in its support of Mitterrand. The CFDT, though clearly favoring the Socialist candidate, was still practicing its distance from electoral politics. It was very different from 1974. Neither of the two unions, nor the employers, seemed to anticipate the victory of Mitterrand. The employers in particular were stunned by the event.[151]

5

Conclusion

Giscard and Barre, whatever the merits of their economic policies, failed to overcome one basic political problem. They were unable to secure a consensus for themselves and their policies: they did not have a political strategy that was viable in the environment of domestic French politics. This was evident in their relations with political parties, the major interest groups, and the electorate.

On the level of political parties, Giscard was unable to secure support for his policy from an important portion of the Gaullists. Much emphasis is usually placed on the personal rivalry between Giscard and Chirac, but this rivalry took place against the background of a very real divergence of views on policy. Giscard's liberal approach contrasted starkly with much of Gaullist ideology and practice. Chirac, it is true, may not have been very strongly committed to Gaullist principles; he may have used the conflict only to promote his own ambitions. (After all, he himself was not very coherent in his thinking on policy.) But then the Gaullists do not owe their political existence to him alone—far from it.

To be sure, this was not the first time that a president

did not get unanimous support from his own "presidential majority" in Parliament. But unlike de Gaulle in the days of Giscard's qualified support and unlike Mitterrand who to some extent does rely on Communist support today, Giscard and his party were not preponderant within the presidential coalition. Even the business world gave Giscard only qualified support by 1981 (with most businessmen preferring Chirac), while the labor unions, not surprisingly, opposed him strongly.

Giscard's coalition in 1974 had depended on Gaullist and Centrist voters for victory. Giscard was able to narrowly defeat Mitterrand in 1974 by absorbing the Centrist votes. By 1981, the marginalization of the Communists on the first ballot, the crisis within the parties on the Right, the bad economic situation, and a desire for change, all played a role in Giscard's defeat. His policy failures pushed the Centrist voters toward Mitterrand. His economic policies and their adverse affect on the new middle class lost Giscard the narrow margin of support that had aided in his 1974 victory.

These circumstances would have been sufficient to make life difficult for any president. The institutions of the Fifth Republic, however, give the president a very special, powerful position. De Gaulle was once confronted with a somewhat similar challenge—hostile interest groups and hostile political parties—during the early years of the Fifth Republic.[152] But de Gaulle took on the challenge by taking his case to the French people, where his support was still overwhelming. Giscard by contrast did not—and could not—undertake a similar effort. He was considerably less popular than either de Gaulle or Pompidou had been, and Barre was by far the most unpopular prime minister the Fifth Republic has yet had.[153] At no time was there a majority to support Barre's economic policies. Typically, they were supported by roughly only one quarter of the electorate, while being rejected by one half or more.[154]

Consistently, a majority of the electorate, in keeping with French tradition, favored an active state role in the economy, whether in the area of employment policy, price controls, or nationalizations.[155] Barre's stance was clearly not in accord with the position of the French electorate. There was irony in this; Giscard had repeatedly proclaimed that France could only be governed from the center, which he wanted to represent. But on economic and social questions, the center was occupied by the Gaullists and the Socialists. Barre's position on the Right fringe was reflected by the position of the Communists on the Left.

Giscard and Barre seemed to take very little notice of these political realities; perhaps they thought that they could brush them off. Barre was correct in assuming that the Gaullists, opposed though they might be to many of the government's policies, would never actually vote against the government if that would threaten the government's existence. He forced the issue on them no less than 10 times by raising the question of confidence with several legislative proposals.[156] Barre also professed total disregard of public opinion surveys. They were traps for the guillible, he said, and did not deserve to be taken seriously.[157] He seemed to think that his own unpopularity was a measure of his merit as prime minister.

What seemed to matter to the president and the prime minister was not whether their government was backed by a unified parliamentary coalition or whether their policies were approved by the people at large. The important point was whether anyone could come up with a viable alternative or whether discontent would become so massive as to wreck governmental policy altogether, as had happened to the austerity policies practiced before May 1968. To Giscard, the breakup of the Left in 1977 and the infighting that followed it showed that such an alternative did not exist in the country. Barre on his side repeatedly pointed to the lack of a massive wave of discontent as evidence of support for his own policies. The 1981 elections showed how much these calculations had become obsolete.

One question remains unclear for the time being. Did Giscard really share the policy orientation of his prime minister without reservations? Just before the 1981 elections, Giscard came up with an employment plan that seemed to conflict with Barre's past policy; he also stated that the greatest misgiving he had about his term in office was not to have dealt with the unemployment problem earlier.[158] But why did he not remove Barre from office? It was widely expected that he might do so to brush up his image before the election. Perhaps he felt that it would have been an injustice; Giscard himself had been treated in a similar way by de Gaulle and had always resented it.[159] But then it is also possible that Giscard did not really want to change his policy course after all.[160] The end came as a surprise—a collapse impressive in its force and swiftness.

II

The Politics of Economic Policy under Mitterrand

6

Socialist Economic Policy

In the first months following President Mitterrand's election in May 1981, there was considerable uncertainty about the policies the Socialists would follow; they had been out of power for too long to have a clear identity, and they had often neglected specifics in their proposals for change.[161] The inclusion of four Communist ministers did not mean that the Common Program of 1972 was to be revived, nor was this politically necessary given the strength of the Socialists, who occupied 285 seats out of 491 in the National Assembly.[162] In fact, to be allowed to join the government, the Communist Party had to accept, on all important questions, the principles laid down by Mitterrand in his presidential platform.

What the Socialists had promised in 1981 can be grouped under two large headings. First, they claimed that they were better qualified to manage the French economy—to bring back growth and a new dynamism, reduce unemployment, and increase investment, while abiding with the basic principles of an internationally open market economy. Second, they promised social reform—changes that would make

French society more just, more humane, and more responsive to the needs and aspirations of its members. The new government began to work on both sets of issues with an impressive amount of energy; even so, the leaders reportedly were frustrated at the slowness of their impact on economic developments. In any case, it was the management of the national economy that enjoyed priority during the first six months of the new government. Although Mitterrand took immediate action on some of his campaign pledges, the flow of most social reforms did not start until 1982, and reforms had to be expedited by recourse to special emergency procedures.

The main themes of Socialist economic policy are growth, renewal, and mobilization of all of France's productive forces. These elements—already part of the Common Program of 1972—acquired particular meaning after the years of relative economic decline after 1974. The core of Socialist policy until the mid-1980s will probably be industrial renewal, not redistribution. Of course redistribution will not be neglected altogether, but for some years to come, it will probably be limited to slow improvements for the lowest income groups and moderate cuts for the upper ranges. The distribution of power will also change somewhat, but not in the radical way demanded by the proponents of *autogestion*.

In chronological terms, the first major policy approach to have an impact on the French economy was the effort to reflate, which lasted from Mitterrand's election to about mid-June 1982, at which time the course was reversed. It is true that the nationalizations were carried out roughly during the same time period, but the actual policy changes resulting from this will not come to be felt fully for several years, when the rapid growth of investments will show its effects. Aid to the private sector will probably take place in a similar time frame.

From Reflation to Austerity

In their economic programs during the 1970s, the Socialists repeatedly advocated a policy of reflation by stimulating demand. In the late 1970s, the emphasis shifted gradually to reflation via investment. But the element of action on the demand side remained important. Once in power, they put into operation a mild reflation; it was to be relayed, they thought, by an increase in exports and investments after the first year. This expectation, however, proved erroneous, as became evident during the first half of 1982.

Critics of the Left—most prominently Barre—had long argued that reflation was bound to fail because reflation would necessarily increase imports, reduce exports, and thus lead to a dramatic balance of payments deficit and a decisive weakening of the franc. The only answer to such a deterioration was either protectionism or austerity. Barre pointed to the *relance Chirac* to illustrate his point.

The Socialists were undaunted by Barre's theories. They thought that they could avoid them by concentrating on particularly labor-intensive sectors and by increasing exports, thanks to a new, more dynamic industrial policy. In addition, they were quite willing to let the franc decline somewhat. They of course also thought that an improvement in the international environment was imminent.

Against this background, government spending was increased immediately after Mitterrand's election. Important social welfare measures were enacted very quickly: pensions and family and housing allowances were increased; new civil service jobs were created; the minimum wage was raised, with the government picking up part of the cost, and the budget deficit was increased and set at nearly 3 percent of the gross domestic product (GDP) for 1982. The reflation did have its expected impact on industrial production, which showed a slight increase in late 1981. But in the spring of 1982, the reflationary approach came to an early end; it became clear that it simply could not be continued any longer. The balance of payments, as predicted by Barre, deteriorated very suddenly in the second quarter of 1982, due to an import surge; the international recession showed no signs of going away; and private investment kept falling, despite the increase in demand. Finally, the inflation in France seemed to accelerate again, whereas it was falling rapidly in most other Organization for Economic Cooperation and Development (OECD) countries.

In May 1982, the tone of governmental pronouncements changed; austerity and sacrifice became key words. In June, Mitterrand made clear at a press conference that the government would concentrate its effort on public sector investment and that this would require containing expenditures on social welfare and other areas.[163] Shortly afterward, the franc was devalued for the second time in less than a year, and a temporary freeze was imposed on prices and wages.[164] (Only the minimum wage was exempted.) In the autumn of 1982, the freeze was scheduled to give way to controlled wage and price movements. Even the government admitted that this could only lead to a reduction of real wages in 1982 and 1983—and in fact, it stressed the need to end the indexation of wages in the public sector. It defended its course by arguing that this was required to free the necessary funds for the extraordinary investment effort of the 1980s. Even so, the event was unprecedented under the Fifth Republic. The austerity attitude of the government was confirmed in September 1982 by the publication of the budget for 1983.[165] Even the new austerity, however, did little to stabilize the franc. In September 1982, there were rumors again of an imminent devaluation, and the government tried to counter the need for it by taking out a $4 billion standby credit, the largest ever granted to a state.[166]

Does this mean that the Socialists intend to practice austerity from now on, that, in other words, they will practice Barre's policy under a different name? Undoubtedly the Socialists are determined to bring down inflation to 10 percent in 1982, and 8 percent in 1983, even at the cost of new hardships. But the long or medium-term perspective of the Socialists is by no means limited to austerity, even if some of them have predicted "three terrible years"—to last until 1985. Although they now admit the existence of an external constraint, the Socialists still argue that a durable expansion is the necessary condition for the realization of socialist goals in the future: higher wages, better welfare programs, better housing, and better education.

To overcome the external constraint, the Socialists have for some time focused on one course of action: the development of a highly advanced industrial sector that would be strongly export-oriented and capable of competing with the industries of the United States, Germany, and Japan—the countries with whom the current trade deficit is greatest. (The French trade surplus, concentrated on Third World countries, is particularly vulnerable at a time when many of those countries are experiencing severe problems of their own.) To develop such a sector is of course the foremost purpose of another major policy approach of the Socialists: nationalization.

Nationalization

The nationalization of banks and major industries was probably the most controversial economic policy measure taken by the new government in its first year of office. Not that there was not a majority to support such a move, but the Right and the majority of the business world regarded the measure as a test of French socialism. If the government backed away from the nationalization program, it would most likely be relatively harmless. On the other hand, if it went through with the program, it was taking the chance of a bureaucratized economy and "collectivism," not to speak of all the uncertainty that would be created during the period of transition when important decisions would presumably be delayed.

The purpose of the nationalization policy had been made quite clear in 1977 in a book by a current Mitterrand adviser, Alain Boublil, entitled *Le socialisme industriel*.[167] Boublil argued that full employment and the equilibrium of international payments could be achieved only if France had a strong, export-oriented industry. This in turn could be achieved only by measures that acted directly on supply, not by stimulation of demand, which resulted only in increased imports. This meant that Keynesianism was largely obsolete.[168]

According to Boublil, the key to success was innovation and investment in industry. Liberal capitalism had failed in this area, mainly because in France it was dominated by finance capitalism (the banks). Finance capital was guided by considerations of short-term profitability. The highest financial rewards in France during the 1970s could be obtained not in industry but in real estate. As a result, most of the bank deposits were channeled into that sector, while industrial investment was neglected. And when the banks did give money to industry, they did so in the form of bonds, not in the form of equity—new issues of stock. This led to rising indebtedness among French industrial firms and squeezed the investors' profits even further. In other words, the banks acted as a parasite, not as a powerful sponsor.[169] Under such conditions it was normal that industrial investments would suffer, something that quickly initiated a vicious circle: lack of investments meant lack of competitiveness, lower profits, and thus even more disinvestment.

Only industrial socialism could reverse this situation,

Boublil argued. It would start out by nationalizing the entire banking sector and a few key industrial firms. Next, it would invest massively in those industries that had been selected for their potential for growth, exports, and employment. In the short run, this would require going against a basic principle of the market economy because investments would be made in sectors that might show a deficit.[170] But profitability, Boublil stressed, was a dynamic notion; it had to be looked at over time. If the firms no longer showed a deficit after a few years, if they could secure a powerful technological monopoly and provide France with exports that were relatively insensitive to international trade fluctuations, then the risk was well worth taking.[171]

On the other hand, Boublil acknowledged that there were limits to what could be done in this way. The state, now the main and most dynamic entrepreneur, also had only limited resources; to subscribe to too massive a program would endanger the success of the whole enterprise. The state therefore had to select a limited range of industries that were particularly promising, either because of technological leadership that would pay off economically, or because of the employment impact or a close relationship with national independence. Boublil also made it clear that any deficit must be temporary; the state must not end up subsidizing obsolete industries.[172] Only concentration of means could bring the desired effect: a breakthrough that would make those industries leaders in the competition for the world market.

Such a program, Boublil argued, was not at all protectionist; on the contrary, it accepted the principle of open borders and even a high level of international trade.[173] But the government had to make certain that France would be placed on an equal level in such trade, instead of falling into the trap of unequal exchange, which could only lead to underdevelopment and national decline.[174] The goal of this policy was to make France a core country in the world political economy, a country that would stand on an equal level with the United States, Germany, and Japan.[175] The main difference between France and the leading capitalist powers would be that in France the advantages of industrial leadership would be reaped by society as a whole, whereas in the other countries they would presumably benefit primarily the multinational corporations. That France would enjoy a consistent balance of trade surplus—something that Boublil specifically mentions—shows that this program, though it is termed socialist and stresses solidarity with the Third World, is predatory in its own way because its realization would mean a concentration of industrial employment in France at the expense of other countries.[176]

Boublil's ideas were widely shared among the Socialist leadership; even Rocard stressed the need for nationalization for similar reasons.[177] If there was agreement on purpose, however, there was no consensus on the modalities. In May and June of 1981, the Socialists were caught somewhat unprepared, partly because their victory had not been entirely expected. There was a lack of experts in the party who were familiar with the companies to be nationalized.[178] Pierre Joxe, the first minister of industry, appointed a commission, headed by Jacques Piette, the man who had already drafted the nationalization program of 1944–1946, to study the problem. Piette apparently prepared a vast program to restructure the French economy into large sectors that would each be dominated by a state-owned company, organized along the lines of Electricité de France, Gaz de France, and Charbonnages de France. This "maximalist" interpretation of Mitterrand's program was soon discarded; its sponsors stepped down quite early.[179] Joxe was then replaced as minister of industry by Pierre Dreyfus, the former chief executive of the state-owned Renault company. A consensus quickly developed among Dreyfus, Mauroy, and the presidential advisers to pattern the industry nationalizations on the highly successful Renault model.[180] The goal would then be strong, competitive firms with a large amount of managerial autonomy, not unwieldly giants like Electricité de France.[181]

But many questions remained. Should the state nationalize the existing companies outright, or should it, as Rocard had argued, merely secure a controlling interest by the acquisition of 51 percent of the capital? The latter method legally was easier: the government could carry it out by buying the shares, or, in the case of heavily indebted firms, by effectively converting its loans into a participation of capital. This would not only save money and legal problems, it would also strengthen the equity basis of the corporations concerned. Finally, in terms of effective control, there would not be all that much difference, Rocard argued, pointing to the French National Railroads, the Société national des chemins de fer français (SNCF), where such a system had long existed.[182]

At the end of the summer of 1981, Mitterrand and Mauroy decided in favor of a 100 percent nationalization for most firms, perhaps as a conciliatory gesture toward the Left wing of the Socialist Party and the Communists, and "to make for a clearer situation" because, clearly, such a step could not be reversed easily.[183] As a result, the measure became much more controversial. The opposition, after proposing a series of amendments in the National Assembly to stall the bill, presented the matter to the Constitutional Council and asked that the law be declared unconstitutional.[184] To the Socialists' relief, the Council—consisting almost entirely of members of the former majority—did not strike the law down; however, it did declare several of its provisions unconstitutional, including the provisions relating to the compensation of shareholders.[185] The government quickly remedied these problems, in particular by the introduction of a new criterion for evaluating the compensation amount, increasing the total compensation by 15 to 20 percent over the previous bill.

When the opposition presented the matter to the Constitutional Council for a second time, its arguments were roundly rejected, and the bill became law with its publication on February 13, 1982. The most important nationalization measure in French history had been enacted; ten leading industrial corporations and all the important banks were placed in public hands.[186] Altogether, the enlarged nationalized sector accounted for 75 percent of all credits and deposits in the banking area; its industrial establishments represented nearly one quarter of all industrial employment, roughly 30 percent of industry's business volume, and 40 percent of all investments.[187]

If there was disagreement on the method, there was a broad consensus on the purpose of nationalization. The close coordination between industry, banks, and the state was to be the basis for a new economic dynamism that would spread throughout the French economy, pulling along a private sector that needed to overcome its hesitations. Such close coordination, Mitterrand explained, was in fact one of the causes of Japan's success.[188] This dynamism was to allow a leap forward comparable to that achieved after the Liberation. Confronted with questions about the rationale for nationalization, many Socialists pointed to the poor investment record of private industry over the preceding decade. Figures show that in the previous ten years, public sector firms increased their investments at an annual rate of about 10 percent (in volume), while in the private sector investment actually decreased. Although public sector investment only represented 18 percent of all gross investment in 1973, the percentage was 32 percent in 1979, but these figures have to be read with some caution.[189]

What the Socialists stressed particularly was the lack of venture capital for industrial investment.[190] Observers sympathetic to the Socialists noted that many industrial firms had adopted very cautious management practices, seeking to improve their financial condition not through an expansion of sales or new product lines but through cutting costs by dismissals and disinvestment. They also noted that many of the banks were unwilling to take on even normal commercial risks.[191] Surprisingly, some of the executives in the targeted industries readily conceded that some definite advantages would result from nationalization; in particular, nationalization would permit a long-term approach to industrial restructuring and free the companies from the constraints imposed by the stock market, the need to show short-term profitability.[192] Most of the executives, with the major exception of Pierre Moussa of Paribas, were in fact quite loyal to the new government, even though most of them knew that they would soon be replaced.[193]

The argument that the newly nationalized firms would become more dynamic under public management was supplemented by another one: that such large concentrations of power in private hands could easily go against the national interest. Mitterrand himself put the matter in very strong terms. Given the phenomenon of increasing accumulation and concentration of capital, he said in his press conference of September 1981, it was only normal that firms that occupy a monopolistic position in the provision of essential goods and services should be nationalized and thus be deprived of their ability to subvert the general interest. Neither private individuals nor foreign interests should occupy key positions in the French economy.[194] To Mitterrand, nationalization represented the famous "break with capitalism" that the Socialists had discussed so much.[195]

Mitterrand's position was not really all that different from that of Rocard or Jacques Delors, who were often portrayed as his opponents on the issue of nationalizations. Both stressed that nationalization would make it possible for the French government to go against policy trends prevailing internationally, to bet on growth and dynamism while other governments and economies retrenched and deflated.[196] Without nationalization, they argued, the firms would in all likelihood act more cautiously, not necessarily out of a desire to undercut the government or its policy. The Barre years had shown that even rising profits were not likely to change this situation. To try to achieve the government's policy goals by regulation and indicative planning would have meant a constant and not very promising struggle.[197] Given the policy goals of the Socialist government, the nationalization measures do not appear as gratuitous or primarily motivated by ideological concerns as some of their adversaries have claimed; they are clearly connected to the "reorientation of the economy,"[198] a goal that includes domestic expansion but also redistribution and many other reforms. Only a more affluent economy could finance all these changes, that was why nationalization was essential.

The nationalization of the banks also must be seen in the same context. The Socialists' main reproach to the banks, as clearly articulated by Boublil, was that they had wasted precious resources on undertakings that, though financially profitable, were nonproductive from the perspective of industry. The nationalization of the banks was intended to induce bankers to take greater risks. Paradoxically, through nationalization the government hoped to make banks act like enterprising capitalists.

The nationalizations were to serve fairly clear objectives set out by the government, and the Socialists' views were clarified when, in early 1982, the new managers were appointed and given their first instructions. Minister of Industry Pierre Dreyfus believed that these executives must share the basic attitude and approach of the government to reduce the need for supervision. The executives appointed in February 1982, remarkable both for their high level of expertise and management experience and by their commitment, in most cases, to the Socialist cause, were given letters stating their mission: to reconcile economic efficiency and social objectives.[199]

The task given the new managers was to preside over France's reindustrialization—reversing the course taken under Barre that led to the loss of 1 million industrial jobs—to maintain normal capital profitability, and to search for greater economic efficiency—not just by cutting costs but by the development of sales and new products and a greater effort at research and innovation. The orientation laid down by the state was to be respected; as to details, the businessmen were to develop a *plan d'entreprise* for each firm that would form a contract with the state.[200] These plans, drawn up for a period of four years, are to be flexible and can be adjusted every year in response to changes in the international environment.[201] Labor Minister Jean Auroux even stated that the firms would be free to dismiss workers in the course of their restructuring process. Nationalized industry was not to become a protected sector that the state would keep alive in the absence of good performance.[202]

Some shadows soon developed over management autonomy. In March 1982, Jean-Pierre Hugon, newly appointed director of the Charbonnages de France, was fired from his post because of his criticism of the government's cutbacks on energy savings to finance the extra cost of Algerian gas. Hugon, the government claimed, had violated his obligation to keep out of political controversy.[203] Two months later, another conflict developed over the question of investments for the public sector. Dreyfus and Delors asked for a large amount to wipe out recent losses in some firms and to broaden the capital base of most of them; they wanted the budget to contribute half of this amount. But Budget Minister Laurent Fabius, concerned about the growing deficit, insisted that the nationalized banks be told to come up with two-thirds of the necessary funds, a proposal that the government finally accepted but one that was hardly compatible with real management autonomy.[204]

The nationalization program was largely completed by early 1982. There remained some questions with regard to those firms on the nationalization list that had passed to a significant degree under foreign control such as Roussel-Uclaf, ITT-France, and CII-Honeywell-Bull. For all of these firms, the idea of a 100 percent nationalization was soon abandoned. Instead, agreements were negotiated with those firms that reduced foreign control in exchange for settlements that were usually quite generous.

Thus the nationalization program was completed in its outline by mid-1982. No firms are to be added to the nationalization list in the near future, except when no private investor can be found to rescue an ailing firm that the government considers important such as the textile manufacturer Boussac-Saint Frères.[205] Mitterrand declared that there would be no "creeping" nationalization and that another expansion of the public sector could only come after the next general election in 1986 or 1988.[206]

But the completion of the nationalization program was only to be the start of a new and very different industrial strategy. The new managers were first asked to come up with ambitious investment plans; they were encouraged to take a bold approach, starting up investment in their firms during the second half of 1982 and continuing it at a rapid pace for several years. The government announced that it would spend about 10 billion francs on the big five industrial companies in 1982 and 1983 and 30 billion francs over the next five years. The total amount of investment for these firms, including resources coming from banks, has been put at 75 billion for the same period.[207] But other firms have also been added; the computer sector alone (essentially CII-Honeywell-Bull) will receive about 2 billion francs before the end of 1983, and a total of 6 billion francs of government funds are programmed until 1986 to make France the third industrial power in the area of microelectronics.[208]

By mid-1982, some doubts arose as to whether all these ambitious investment programs could be maintained. Would the new emphasis on austerity and a limited budget deficit in 1983 not present insurmountable financing problems?[209] If there were severe cutbacks, then the main justification for the nationalizations would have evaporated. Initial statements by Socialist leaders indicated that industrial investment, in particular in the nationalized sector, would have priority.[210] In fact, the need to save resources for investment may have been one of the major reasons for the austerity program submitted by the Socialist government in June 1982.

When can we judge whether nationalization has been a success? Every firm is to concentrate on major lines of production, breaking with the diversification of previous years, and this restructuring and investment will need to go on for several years. The government itself declared that the results of the new nationalizations would show by 1986—at the time of the next elections to the National Assembly.[211]

Policy toward the Private Sector

Nationalization was not the only measure intended to revitalize the French economy; the private sector was also to be given a boost. At the outset, however, the attitude of the Socialists toward the private sector was ambiguous. These firms were viewed as bastions of capitalism and a likely place for the class struggle to take place. From this perspective, it seemed appropriate to impose new taxes on business profits. On the other hand, business cooperation was clearly necessary for the government to succeed with its economic policy, and both Mitterrand and Mauroy avoided discouraging business, stressing that their policy of growth would have beneficial effects for business as well. The conflict between the two attitudes came out clearly when the Socialist Party, at its Valence party congress in the autumn of 1981, used radical antibusiness rhetoric. Mitterrand and Mauroy quickly made it clear that this did not reflect the policy orientation of the government.[212]

There were several ways in which public policy was intended to help business performance. In the autumn of 1981, a whole series of financial incentives were incorporated in the 1982 budget. By the end of that year, the first projects for recapturing the French market were announced. In April 1982, important concessions to business were made with regard to tax breaks and social welfare contributions. Nationalization of the banks was followed by measures designed to facilitate credit procedures and by instructions to the banks to be more entrepreneurial in their management practices.[213] Efforts were made to channel investment capital into industry, and in September 1982 the applicability of the wealth tax to business firms was suspended until 1985.[214]

The financial incentives to private sector firms contained in the 1982 budget were numerous; the Socialists pointed out proudly that they brought a 52 percent increase of such aid over the previous year.[215] But the difference with earlier budgets was not only in the volume of the allocated funds, the new criteria for receiving such funds were considerably more selective. Replacement investments, which had become the prevailing form of investment during the Barre years, often with the effect of reducing unemployment, were no longer subsidized.[216] The government placed special emphasis on helping small and medium-sized businesses, hoping that this sector would be particularly cooperative—a hope that early on proved unrealistic.[217] Other measures encouraged the formation of equity capital. Small savers were encouraged by the institution of a passbook with a higher rate of interest. Even the wealth tax was designed to encourage investment, though that was hardly its primary purpose. The creation of new firms was also encouraged in several ways.[218] Finally, the government repeatedly reduced interest rates until the speculation against the franc in the spring of 1982 forced it to reverse its course. The Socialists also argued very strongly that the countries of the European Community should take a common stand and defend themselves against the high U.S. interest rates or France would adopt such a course on its own.[219]

The business world, and particularly the employers' CNPF, showed little enthusiasm for most of these measures. They claimed that the government in fact took more from private firms in the form of additional taxes than it returned in increased subsidies. They claimed that the single most important measure to help business would be to stabilize or reduce business payments to the state in the form of taxes and social welfare contributions. In particular, they asked for a suppression of the *taxe professionnelle* (a kind of business and occupation tax, the shortcomings of which were openly admitted by the government) and of the wealth tax.

After several months of dialogue, the Socialist government made important concessions in April 1982. It committed itself to reduce the *taxe professionelle* by 5 billion francs in 1982 and by another 6 billion francs in 1983, to take over the financing of programs for the handicapped (saving business another 7 billion), not to increase social welfare contributions until mid-1983, and not to reduce the legal work week below the 39-hour limit introduced in early 1982 until the end of 1983. In exchange for this, the head of the employer organization promised that business would perform on investment and hiring.[220] The wealth tax on business was also suspended in September 1982.

The "reconquest of the internal market" was invoked frequently in Socialist programs in the 1970s, though for a long time there was considerable uncertainty as to what this could mean given the fact that the Socialists also declared their opposition to protectionism. In September 1981, a first illustration of this reconquest was given in the furniture sector. An agreement was worked out between French producers, distributors, and the state to limit imports, which were programmed to fall from 21 percent to 15 percent of French sales in one year. Given the expectation of greater domestic sales, the producers could now expand and modernize production with much greater confidence. State aid for investment and research and development would also assist them, which might mean a currency savings of 1 billion francs. The consensus of all the participants was secured quite easily, and by January 1982 the business paper *Les Echos* reported that the climate in this particular industry had improved remarkably.[221]

Similar plans were soon drawn up for other sectors. The machine tool industry is important for most advanced industrial countries. In France, however, it never developed very far, and under Giscard the industry had been shrinking steadily. In early December 1981, Pierre Dreyfus announced a plan to strengthen it. Production was to be doubled in three years, import penetration reduced from 60 percent to 30 percent, and exports increased from 15 percent to 35 percent. Given the rapid, worldwide increase in the use of industrial robots, the stakes are high. The government is to help in a variety of ways: by organizing specialization and competition, encouraging standardization and research, assisting with the training of specialized labor, offering contracts for the development of prototypes, and using the purchasing power of the public sector.[222]

Comparable plans followed for the textile industry—where 250 thousand jobs (30 percent of the total) had been lost over the previous 10 years—for the leather industry, for the toy industry, and for the merchant marine, and more are on the drawing board.[223] What these plans have in common is a determination to recapture French markets for domestic producers by measures that combine great inventiveness with remarkable flexibility. The problems of each sector are dealt with individually. There is no standardized prescription that applies to every situation. It is remarkable that in most of these cases private industry was unable to take the initiative in working out such plans.

In addition to these measures, the government is singling out industry for privileged treatment in other ways. Jean-Pierre Chevènement, appointed minister of industry in addition to his research portfolio in the summer of 1982, put great emphasis on expanding the French research budget, which is expected to grow 18 percent every year in real terms until 1985.[224] He wants to see close cooperation between private and public researchers and business firms. He also stressed the need to free industry from price controls as early as possible. The government indeed promised that industry would receive favored treatment in the period of "negotiated" price controls that is to follow the freeze of 1982.[225]

When can we judge whether Socialist economic policy is a success? The austerity policy will have to last at least until the end of 1983, perhaps longer, to produce the expected reduction of inflation and of the balance of trade deficit. If the reluctant consent of unions, business, and the Communist Party can be secured or if there is at least no major explosion, that policy should bear fruit. Recapturing French market shares will take longer. We will have to wait until after 1985 to see whether the massive investments that are to rebuild the nationalized industries will actually take place. Even then it may take several more years before we can know if the goal of nationalization—the lifting of external constraints—can be achieved. Clearly an unfavorable international environment during much of the 1980s would mean that conflict with the leading industrial powers cannot be avoided. The outcome of such rivalries is necessarily uncertain.

7

Social Reforms

One of the major claims of the Socialists was that they would be able to manage the economy more successfully, even by the traditional standards such as growth, investment, and the balance of payments. They have also claimed that they could reshape economic and social life and make French society more just, more humane, and more responsive to the aspirations of the French. Socialist economic growth would correct injustices in the distribution of material burdens and benefits, provide new solidarity in the face of unemployment, transfer much social control back to the people, and develop a new way of life—one more convivial and spontaneous—that would deemphasize the competitive and individualistic consumption of material goods and would lead to the development of a new community.

Redistribution of Income and Wealth

During the second half of the 1970s, for the first time, poverty and inequality received much attention in France. A much-debated OECD report published in 1976 showed that France was remarkable among industrial countries both for its great inequalities and its high incidence of poverty.[226] Some steps to correct this situation had in fact been taken in the wake of the upheavals of 1968. For some time the minimum wage had increased more rapidly than average hourly wages, and even the Barre government had proclaimed that the lowest income groups must fare better than the others in times of austerity. However, this had only led to relatively modest changes.[227]

The Common Program of the Left in 1972 contained a massive plan for income redistribution. But as the 1970s wore on, it became clear that the program, built on the assumption of record growth rates, was becoming increasingly incompatible with the deteriorating economic situation. In response to this, the Socialists (but not the Communists) adjusted their proposals. The measures taken by the Socialist government since 1981 show considerable moderation. Several measures have been taken on the redistribution of income, the most important ones concerning the increase of the minimum wage, family and housing allowances, and retirement pensions. Minimum wages were increased by 10 percent in June 1982, but this was a modest increase when compared to the massive increases granted in 1934 and 1968 —and considerably less than what the Communists demanded. The government also made it clear that it did not want to see this increase replicated throughout the wage hierarchy. As a result, the measure reached a comparatively small percentage of wage earners.[228] For 1982, the French minimum wage was programmed to increase another 5 percent (or 7.6 percent if one took into account the reduction of working hours without reduction of salary). This move was not affected by the austerity package of June 1982, which specifically exempted the minimum wage.[229]

In general, the government supports wage settlements that will reduce the gap between low and high wages and has shown the way in the area of civil service pay.[230] But average real wages will at best rise slowly, held down by two main constraints. The first is the need to absorb unemployment; higher wage costs reinforce the trend to replace labor with capital. The other constraint (related to the first) is the reduction of working hours, especially the reduction of the work week from 40 to 39 hours, which became law in early 1982. (Further reductions are planned.) Wages will rarely be reduced; this in turn means that the hourly cost of labor is increased already, with its attendant, and negative, effect on job creation.[231]

Family allowances were increased more drastically (25 percent in June 1981 and another 25 percent in February 1982), as were other allowances and pensions, which taken together reach a large number of the needy.[232] In this area, however, further progress seemed unlikely after June 1982; future increases will simply keep up with inflation, at least as long as the climate of austerity continues. With regard to social security, the government rejected the idea proposed by Minister of National Solidarity Nicole Questiaux that the state budget should take over a growing share of the rapidly increasing expenses. Because employer contributions are already very high (and thus discourage hiring), and are not to be raised until 1983, the most likely answer to the threatening deficit will be increased contributions by wage earners as well as curtailed benefits.[233]

Another way in which the government has acted on the distribution of income and wealth is the tax system. The first tax reforms of the Socialist government affect redistribution in several ways. A wealth tax has been introduced on assets exceeding 3 million francs, with a tax rate ranging from 0.5 to 1.5 percent. Despite campaign statements by Mitterrand to the contrary, business property will also be taxed, though exemption is possible if profits are reinvested.[234] Taxes for high incomes were increased by adding another tax bracket at the upper end, putting the highest bracket up from 60 percent to 65 percent. Another measure directed at the higher incomes called for the taxation of business expense accounts. Finally, a limit was also placed on the tax advantages granted for taxpayers' dependents—but this was reversed later on. These reforms fell somewhat short of the grand design to shift to a much greater reliance on direct taxes; in fact, the Socialists even increased the sales tax (the taxe sur la valeur ajoutée—the TVA), and a campaign promise to abolish it completely on essential goods was only partially realized. Once these projects are implemented, they will last for the duration of Mitterrand's term in office; at least that is what the government promised.[235] Thus the scope of change is already fairly clear. Clear, too, is that some of the measures adopted to encourage the formation of risk capital are likely to benefit the wealthy, though it is true that Mitterrand also created a savings booklet for small, low-income savers with a guaranteed, indexed return.[236]

Unemployment Policy

Since 1974, increases in the productivity of labor had been greater than increases in production. As a result, despite continued, if slow, economic growth, the total number of hours worked decreased each year, with the single exception of 1976.[237] This falling demand for labor coincided with the arrival of unusually large numbers of persons on the labor market, hence a rapidly growing unemployment problem.

Reflation and capital-intensive reindustrialization could never by themselves absorb the labor force, which will grow at a rapid rate every year until 1985. One plausible approach then would be to reduce the duration of the working hours of each wage earner. (Under Barre, the previous trend toward a shrinking work week had virtually come to a halt.) This reduction could spread employment more evenly throughout the population, particularly if wage costs were to remain unaffected.

The most important measure that the Socialists had proposed in this context was the gradual reduction of the work week to 35 hours by 1985.[238] A first step was negotiated between business and labor in July 1981; it reduced the work week to 39 hours and introduced a fifth week of vacation on a general basis. The French Employers' Association, the CNPF, and most unions signed the agreement, although the CGT refused, demanding an immediate reduction to 38 hours. The results of the negotiations were sanctioned by a law that authorized the government to implement this agreement by decree; the corresponding *ordonnance* became effective in February 1982.[239] The decree was immediately followed by strikes and controversy: Would the reduction of work be accompanied by at least a partial reduction of wages, or would salaries remain untouched? The decree itself provided for "full compensation" (that is, no reduction in wages) only for those earning the minimum wage; otherwise the details were to be worked out by the social partners.

Many members of the government, however, were at first clearly in favor of a partial reduction of wages. Prime Minister Mauroy, Minister of the Economy Delors, Labor Minister Auroux, Planning Minister Rocard, and others argued that the reduction of the work week had to be accompanied by a partial reduction in wages if the desired effect on employment (that is, new hiring) was to be achieved. Otherwise the reduction of working time would simply benefit those who already had a job and increase the financial burden on business, which would then be unable to increase employment.[240] In fact, several agreements negotiated before February 1982, especially in the building and construction sector, provided for some adjustment of wages due to the new work week.[241] But then Mauroy began to waver, and eventually Mitterrand made a statement that an actual reduction of wages should only be considered once the reductions reached a certain threshold (for example, 37 hours). Until then, he stated, no worker should fear for his income on account of the 39-hour week.[242]

The state showed the way: in the public sector, reduced hours were not accompanied by a corresponding wage adjustment. These statements and practices made further negotiations between unions and employers more difficult, however. It was less likely that unions would accept pay cuts under those circumstances, even though some union leaders, most prominently Edmond Maire, had in fact argued for such cuts earlier on.[243] Nevertheless, several such agreements were signed.[244] Mitterrand's decision was viewed essentially as political—he would not be outbid on his left by the Communists, especially such a short time before the regional elections.[245]

The 39-hour week was undoubtedly popular; as a job-creation measure or as an embodiment of solidarity in the face of rising unemployment, however, it was a failure. It will probably create no jobs; in fact, it made labor still more expensive, thus encouraging its substitution by capital. Shortly after its introduction, the government agreed in April 1982 not to reduce the legal work week before the end of 1983.[246] This left the field open for negotiations, but the 35-hour week by 1985 seemed now in doubt.

The government also acted to reduce working time in January 1982 by issuing a decree that created financial incentives for firms to conclude "solidarity contracts" (*contrats de solidarité*) that would introduce part-time work, reduce work to 37 hours or less by January 1983, or allow retirement even before the age of 60, provided that these measures had a counterpart in the creation of new jobs.[247] By the end of April 1982, close to 2,000 such contracts had been signed. Nearly all of them provided for earlier retirement;

only a few introduced the reduction of work time. Altogether they resulted in the creation of somewhat more than 31 thousand jobs. More than 3,000 solidarity contracts were still being negotiated at that time.[248]

The government also encouraged the introduction of part-time work in other ways. For the civil service it proposed the introduction of a four-day week and of half-time work, with salary cuts of 20 percent and 50 percent respectively.[249] But much remained to be done in this area. Within the European Community, France has the lowest rate of part-time work; just to catch up with the European average would, according to the claims of a former planning commissioner, result in the creation of 1 million jobs.[250] This would reduce unemployment by perhaps 500 thousand—a substantial contribution to solving the unemployment problem. (The formula would also increase the number of job seekers.) Perhaps a more flexible approach is necessary in addition to the *contrats de solidarité*. For executives and supervisory personnel in private business the government proposed a "sabbatical year" formula; on such a leave, the *cadres* would also be encouraged to create an enterprise of their own.

An additional measure intended to free jobs throughout the economy was introduced by yet another decree in March 1982. The right to retire at age 60 seems to be important and welcome to nearly all Frenchmen.[251] In fact, it is a right that already exists for many wage earners in both the public and private sectors, often under special arrangements for specific situations. In addition, since 1972 all wage earners dismissed after the age of 60 can claim 70 percent of their last salary (the *garantie de ressources*). This was extended in 1977 to those who resigned voluntarily. Thus the great majority of Frenchmen already had the right to retire at the age of 60 or earlier in some cases. However, these schemes were based on agreements between employers and wage earners (with the state also making a financial contribution) that were always limited in time. The current agreement expires in early 1983.

Mauroy promised that under the new regulation everyone would have the right to retire at age 60 with 70 percent of his or her salary. But, in fact, the government by itself can only come up with 50 percent of the salary, which is to be paid out of the social security system. The remainder will come from supplementary retirement funds. The amount to be paid out of these funds still needs to be negotiated, with groups such as employers and the various unions taking very different positions so far.[252] Under these circumstances and given the new financial austerity, the reform of the retirement system is likely to have only a limited impact on the job situation.

A more radical approach to the unemployment problem, advocated by some experts of the National Institute of Statistics and Economic Studies would be to manipulate the cost of the factors of production (capital and labor) to make the recourse to labor more attractive than the recourse to investment, at least within certain ranges and during periods of high unemployment.[253] For decades, the state has granted incentives to investment, thus reducing the effective cost of capital. Since the beginning of the economic crisis, the French state has also—de facto—taxed employment and thus discouraged the use of labor because social welfare contributions in France are largely paid by employers, more so than in most other Common Market countries.[254] When unemployment went up, the contributions went up as well, making labor even more expensive and thus encouraging its substitution by capital, clearly a vicious circle.[255] Wage increases and full compensation for the 39-hour week only compounded the problem. For the individual firm, the decisive economic elements are the relative costs of capital and labor, but for the national economy as a whole, it is a different set of figures that is relevant. Labor is not "saved" when in fact it has to be paid for out of unemployment compensation funds, not to speak of political commitments to reduce the ranks of the jobless.

To encourage the use of labor, it is not necessary to hold down real wages, though this is what conservative politicians usually recommend. The state could correct the situation that results from the distorted costs of labor and capital and renders impossible their optimum use by taxing investment and using the proceeds to subsidize labor, for example, by taking over part of the social welfare contributions. To be sure, there are important limitations; the goal is to reach the optimum level for the use of both capital *and* labor.[256] In any case, the Socialists, like previous governments, have continued to subsidize investment in a variety of ways, and have taken only timid steps toward reducing the cost of labor. Thus the *Pacte National pour l'Emploi*, introduced by Barre to subsidize the employment of mostly young people, has been continued and broadened as the *Plan Avenir Jeunes*.[257] For the particularly labor-intensive textile industry, the government has consented—under certain conditions—to take over part of the employers' social welfare contributions for a limited period.[258] But there seems to be no intention of expanding this approach to the economy as a whole. The pause in social welfare contributions announced in April 1982, however, and the simultaneous tax breaks for business with regard to the *taxe professionnelle*, may be somewhat related to this approach.

Several other measures were taken in the effort to bring unemployment under control. Civil service jobs were created largely as promised. An effort was made to better adapt the supply of labor to demand, such as a plan to guarantee vocational training for all 16-18 year olds who are no longer in school.[259] This measure will probably only show its effects over time. For the immediate future, the Socialists have accepted the idea that they cannot yet put a halt to unemployment. In April 1982, Labor Minister Auroux stated that he expected the creation of about 100 thousand jobs thanks to the *contrats de solidarité* by the end of 1982 and almost no effect at all from the introduction of the 39-hour week.[260] In May, he announced that unemployment compensation would have to be decreased in the future.[261]

Except for the CFDT, the labor unions were not exactly eager to contribute much to a policy of greater solidarity of wage earners in the face of unemployment. However, their acceptance—or perhaps, more appropriately, toleration—of wage controls, which clearly could only mean a loss of purchasing power, will help to promote employment relative to investment and thus should contribute to the absorption of unemployment. The public sector unions' reaction to an unemployment contribution is similar.

Autogestion?

In their programs during the 1970s, the Socialists stressed that they would also change the structure of power in society, particularly in business firms. This structure they blamed for many evils of capitalist society. The leading slogan in this context was *autogestion* (self-management socialism), a word that lent itself to many quite different interpretations.

But once the Socialists came to power *autogestion* was soon downplayed. A report on the right of wage earners, the *rapport Auroux,* was approved relatively late, in March 1982. The legislation derived from it, to be enacted in the autumn of 1982, endeavors to make labor relations more contractual, rather than hierarchical, and greatly expands the rights of labor unions. In many ways, France is catching up with the legislation of the New Deal or similar laws enacted in much of Western Europe after World War II. Despite the limited scope of this legislation, many employers were quite upset about it; they think that new conflicts will result. In any case, it is clear that the *lois Auroux* will fall far short of codetermination along German or Swedish lines and will in no way even approach self-management socialism. In fact, some members of the government see in the *lois Auroux* a piece of social engineering that should greatly increase the economic efficiency of the French business enterprise.[262]

In a related area, the Socialist government turned out to be far more conservative than some militants had expected. In opposition, the Socialist Party had made vague promises about a new model of economic development, particularly with regard to energy where the Socialists said they would reduce the role of nuclear power. But within months of their rise to power, they reversed themselves on this issue and pushed a large nuclear program through the National Assembly. The rationale: it was good for France to have surplus nuclear capacity so that economic expansion would not be restrained by possible bottlenecks in the energy sector.[263] The earlier objections of the candidate Mitterrand and many other prominent Socialists were simply swept under the rug. The main goal of the Socialist government now is to succeed in very traditional economic terms, surely no easy task in itself. Earlier questions about the ecological and human dimensions of economic development—questions taken up in particular by the *autogestion* wing of the party—are not likely to become important during the next few years and indeed are not the primary concerns of the current leadership.

8

Problems and Prospects

French national politics, particularly at election time, traditionally revive old fears on both the Left and the Right. A whole host of monsters then comes to haunt the French political imagination. For the Right, the prospect of a victory by the Left always conjures up a series of threats. Many on the Right have argued over the last decade that the Communists would quickly come to dominate the Socialists, thanks to the Communists' effective control over the largest union (the CGT).[264] Another fear was that radicals in or outside labor unions might mobilize the workers and ask for a fundamental change in wages and working conditions along the lines of 1936 and 1968.[265] In the high-level negotiations between business, labor, and the government in the wake of such a mobilization, a leftist government might surrender to demagogic demands and effectively wreck the French economy for a long time to come.

Even if that catastrophe were avoided, a leftist government in which the Communists had a decisive voice might do much the same thing in a year or two. Irresponsible expenditures by the Left would increase inflation to unprecedented levels, imports would increase dramatically and exports decline because of lack of competitiveness, and soon the government would find itself forced to resort to strong protectionist measures that could only aggravate the problem. This would, within a few years, leave an economy bled white by excessive wage and social welfare payments, indebted internationally, and only artificially maintained by ever-increasing state intervention.

These fears of the Right are based in part on the conservative interpretation of the record of leftist governments in French history, and it is true that the *Cartel des Gauches* in 1924 and the *Front Populaire* in 1936-1937 ended in economic failure. However, the reasons for their failure were not necessarily (and certainly not exclusively) the ones the Right likes to focus on.

These rightist fears have their counterpart on the Left. There, the favorite specter is the sabotage of progressive governmental policies by business or the owners of capital. The Left believes businessmen lack all patriotic sense, are prepared to move their capital abroad at the first opportunity, will halt all investment and hiring, and will generally paralyze public policy to bring down a leftist government as quickly as possible. They will even—so goes the fear—inflict losses upon themselves as long as they can damage the government.

With these fears in mind, we now can ask questions about the Socialist government. Are the Socialists likely to be successful with their economic and social policies? Will they be able to maintain sufficient political support among the major groups and organizations of the country and among the public? Will they be successful in confronting the international environment and will their policies be successful in economic terms?

Dangers on the Left

The Socialist government may conceivably encounter several dangers because of political problems with the Left. The danger most stressed by the Right before the elections was that of the Socialists being swamped either by a strong Communist partner perhaps backed up by an uncontrollable radical element among the new Socialist deputies or by a popular mobilization movement along 1936 or 1968 lines. In the first year of the Socialist government, none of these dangers seemed likely. Not that the Socialist government did not experience problems with the parties and labor unions that make up the Left, but the problems were of a different nature. What the Socialists complained about most was a lack of support for the government among the labor unions and apathy and disunity on the Left.

Even observers sympathetic to the Left had in the past stressed the problem of a "Communist threat." But that threat had diminished considerably in the late 1970s, and this was confirmed by the results of the 1981 elections. In electoral terms, the Communist Party reached a catastrophic low in 1981 (15.3 percent of the vote in the presidential elections; 16.17 percent in the subsequent National Assembly elections), and the number of Communist deputies had fallen from 86 to 44.[266] The party did not show any signs of recovery in the 1982 regional elections, where it again won only 15.87 percent of the vote.[267] To have four Communist ministers in the government, the Communist Party had virtually to capitulate, condemning most of its recent foreign policy stand and binding Communists to loyal cooperation with the government at all levels. Even Communist labor had to accept and respect "the choice of May 10."[268]

In general, the four Communist ministers have been models of loyalty, but the Communist Party leaders clearly practice a two-faced policy: cooperation with the Socialists, whom, from 1977 to 1981, the Communists had denounced as social democratic traitors, concurrently with a purge in the party and the CGT of those who, after the break of 1977, continued to advocate continued unity and cooperation between Socialists and Communists. From this, it is not altogether farfetched to infer that the Communist Party is preparing for the possibility of renewed confrontation.

Although the Socialists do not need Communist support at the present time in the National Assembly, the CGT remains the most important labor union. As long as there is the possibility that the Communist leadership could effectively use the union to destabilize the government, the Socialist leadership must remain wary. At present, the decline of the Communist Party has been paralleled by a decline of the CGT in union elections, in membership, in militancy, and in revenues.[269] More important perhaps, the union is profoundly divided over political questions, as happened when the leaders used the unions to promote the candidacy of Georges Marchais in the presidential election.[270] Dissent intensified during the summer and fall of 1981, when the Communist Party moved to consolidate its hold over the executive organs of the union, resulting in the resignations of two high-level leaders. Not since 1966 had such high-level dissent occurred in the union, a dissent that reached new and unprecedented levels during the Polish crisis in late 1981, when the CGT was the only labor union not to condemn General Wojciech Jaruzelski's crackdown on Solidarity.[271] Discipline within the organization nearly collapsed; whole federations sent in their collective protests.[272] Although the leadership within the party and the union soon reasserted itself and produced a show of relative unity, the real problems at issue were avoided.[273]

After June 1981, many political observers predicted that the Communist Party and the CGT were unreliable allies who would aggressively oppose the Socialist government if it either experienced economic difficulties or shifted toward a policy of austerity. Mitterrand's statement on the 39-hour week—that no wage earner should fear his wages despite the 1-hour reduction—was seen as a concession to the CGT, which strongly opposed anything but full compensation. On the occasion of the *pause Mauroy*, the CGT predictably protested against these "free gifts" to business. But when, in June 1982, austerity became the official policy of the government, the Communists soon pledged their support as long as wage earners would not be alone in carrying the necessary burdens.[274] In late summer 1982, the Communists even called upon the workers to mobilize for the great battle of production to help the government succeed. The last time the Communists had taken such a step was almost 40 years ago, immediately after the Liberation.

For the Communists, it is clearly the CGT, which is under Communist hegemony, though not under exclusive Communist control, that is potentially the greater problem. It is less troubled than the Communist Party and still remains France's largest labor union. With regard to Socialist support, the problem is different. When the Socialists triumphed in the parliamentary elections of June 1981, a large contingent of new deputies entered the National Assembly. Many of them were teachers who often lacked a background in economics and—as intellectuals—were suspected of a penchant for dogmatism. In fact, the government was somewhat concerned at first about its own majority and decided to "channel" its self-expression.[275] In this effort the Socialist leadership was largely successful; there were not too many instances of radical rhetoric, except during the Valence party congress in the fall of 1981 and during the debate on the policy of nationalization.

On the whole, however, it does not seem as though the Socialist Party's parliamentary delegation exercised much influence on the formulation of governmental policy. It was somewhat taken aback by the *pause Mauroy* and criticized the *pause* for lacking solid counterparts in the form of tangible business concessions, but received little satisfaction. It was also largely ignored when the government submitted the *lois Auroux;* the Socialist deputies would undoubtedly have gone substantially further in their reforms than the government.[276] On the occasion of the major policy change of June 1982, a scheduled consultation with the party was postponed until the decisions were taken. The Socialists had little choice but to acquiesce, despite a reluctance to do so in certain quarters.[277]

If the Socialist Party did not make a stronger show of power in its first year after the 1981 elections, this is in part due to the institutions of the Fifth Republic; it is also due to the particular state in which the party found itself. Undoubtedly, the Socialists have suffered from the fact that most of their major leaders were now in government and no longer retained party functions. Militantism also fell after the elections, and more difficult times may yet occur because of the mid-1982 call for understanding and sacrifice.[278] At Valence, the party defined its own role as that of a "force of proposition, impulsion, and reflection."[279] The government sees things somewhat differently, however; it now wants the party to explain official policy and has criticized it for not living up to this task.[280]

Leftist parties and unions can create serious difficulties for a Socialist government by overloading it with excessive demands and by resisting changes that may be required to overcome crises. With unemployment in France reaching important proportions, the government has relied heavily on a reduction of working hours and has urged greater solidarity among all its citizens. That policy can only be successful if wage earners are prepared to accept a wage evolution that would take into account the reduction of working hours and something less than the "full compensation" the government originally proposed. But from the outset, two of the three largest unions, the CGT and the reformist Force ouvrière simply rejected such an approach out of hand.[281] The result—reduced hours with full pay—did improve the situation of those who were employed, but did little if anything for the unemployed. Of the major unions, only the CFDT, long the strongest advocate of solidarity among all workers without regard to their status, took a different stand.

In its first year in office, the Socialist government did not follow a clear policy toward the unions. It avoided singling out any one union for special treatment. At first, the Socialists seemed to share the approach of the CGT, which repeatedly opposed any policy of austerity. Only during the spring of 1982 did the government move more closely to the position of the CFDT. However, when in June 1982 the policy of austerity was proclaimed, all three major unions seemed prepared to cooperate, at least for a while, and most strikes in 1981–1982 were called not by the union leadership, but by local units.

As to the danger that the Socialist government may have to face a mass mobilization that could only be settled by giving into excessive demands, one has to remember that twice in this century—in 1936 and 1968—France has seen such a phenomenon. It should be noted in both cases, however, the movement was directed against a government of the Right, and in both cases the unions played essentially a stabilizing role. Nonetheless, many observers expected another such mobilization to take place after the victory of Mitterrand in 1981 and were surprised when it did not.

Mobilization is even less likely to occur after the Socialists' first year in office. The government's pragmatic search for improvement responds to many aspirations, but there is little now to encourage the nearly utopian expectations that seem to have been characteristic of 1936 and 1938. New occasions for turmoil and mobilization certainly may arise, but mobilization is more likely to be a spontaneous phenomenon, not one that can easily be predicted.

In any case, the prospect for such a mass movement is never entirely absent from the French political scene. Employers especially are nervous and see dangers in fairly small incidents. After all, had not the Socialist Party at Valence announced a possible "radicalization" of the struggle in the enterprises to make employers more pliant?

The government certainly would have liked to receive more union support for its own policy and did encourage the unions to become more active. But this has little to do with a mass mobilization. More cooperation was the government's goal, not a radicalization, which, unlike the Socialist Party, it had never advocated. Even this limited goal is not likely to be achieved in the near future, however. The major unions do not want to be associated too closely with the Socialist government. The CGT wants to preserve its separate identity and hold the fort in the hope of a revival of the Communist Party. The CFDT stresses that governmental policy alone is not sufficient to bring about change and that social movements must play a major and relatively independent role. The Force ouvrière, while friendly toward the Socialist government, does not want to get into politics and does not want to compromise union independence.

For the Socialists in power, this situation is clearly disappointing. They had hoped that the unions would support their major goals and mobilize the world of labor on behalf of governmental policies.[282] Instead, they find organizations that are somewhat cooperative, yet maintain a critical distance. It must be added that union agreement with governmental policy would have been a difficult feat under any circumstances, as the unions disagree among themselves on very important points.[283] Clearly, any hope for a united labor front is misplaced.

The government certainly faces problems on the Left. But these problems are unlike the dramatic threats projected by the Right before the elections and closely resemble the problems that any government would face in times of economic difficulties. In some respects, and in one of those paradoxes not infrequent in politics, the Socialist government is probably better placed to ask the Left for sacrifices than would be a government of the Right.[284]

Dangers on the Right

On the other side of the political spectrum, the government is faced with related kinds of problems. There is the possible threat of sabotage by business, or at least of a cooperation so hesitant or so reluctant that major policy objectives cannot be achieved. Second, the political parties of the Right might stage such a strong comeback that the government would appear ineffective. If public opinion should massively desert the Socialist government, it would suffer a serious setback.

There have been several occasions in French history on which businessmen (or the holders of capital) have withheld their performance or cooperation; not surprisingly, this was most dramatic under governments of the Left. There was substantial capital flight after the formation of the government of Edouard Herriot in 1924.[285] But the most decisive episode took place after the victory of the Popular Front in 1936 when a massive capital flight was followed by an equally massive investment strike. The determination to sabotage the government was quite clear.

It is this history that has shaped the views of many people on the Left, and indeed the possibility of business sabotage of governmental policies cannot be ruled out. But the current situation is different from 1936 in more than one respect. Even if there were an effort at such sabotage, its possibilities would be considerably restricted compared to the days of the Popular Front. The exchange control legislation that Blum failed to obtain has been in place long since, even under conservative governments, and the outgoing Barre government exercised tight supervision during its last days in power.[286] There was some capital flight, but only on a limited scale, and the Socialists have lifted the anonymity that had governed all transactions in gold.[287] In addition, the nationalization policy restricts the possibilities of sabotage. It makes a united front of business against government far more difficult.

Is there in fact a will to sabotage the policies of Mitterrand and the Socialist government on the part of French business? Immediately after the elections there were clearly some entrepreneurs who wanted to do everything possible to bring down the new government.[288] Lagging cooperation with the government's attempts to start up hiring and investment was evident in later months as well, though it is not clear to what extent the reasons were purely economic, as businessmen usually claimed.[289] It does seem that businessmen made a show of studied pessimism, painting reality in excessively dark colors and thus discouraging hiring and investment.[290] On the occasion of the Valence party congress, with its denunciations of business and its class rhetoric, many thought they had seen the writing on the wall.[291] Hardliners in the CNPF wanted systematic opposition to the government. However, the election of Yvon Gattaz to the leadership of the CNPF, in December 1981, indicated that they were in a minority, as Gattaz stands for a progressive group of employers and is known to favor dialogue with the Socialist government.[292]

The Moussa affair, in the fall of 1981, offered a test of the loyalty of big business. Pierre Moussa headed the Banque de Paris et des Pays-Bas (Paribas), and, in order to protect some of the international holdings of his firm from nationalization, he made the French bank lose majority control over its Swiss subsidiary. Even though this was not illegal—a decree outlawing such actions was passed only shortly afterwards—it clearly undercut the policy of the government. In this situation, it was the board of Paribas, which lists some of France's most prominent industrialists, that forced Moussa's resignation, declaring that it would respect the policy of a democratically elected government.[293] It was a far cry from 1936, when some businessmen said that they would rather have Hitler than Blum.[294]

On the other hand, French businessmen were clearly unhappy with the general direction of the government's economic and social policies, and they were particularly upset with that policy under the special conditions prevailing in 1981-1982, at the bottom of the recession. At first, they criticized the unstable conditions for business brought about by such measures as nationalization, the wealth tax, the budget deficit, and the like. Clearly those criticisms did not have much —if any—impact. But soon business focused its complaints on the new financial burdens that business firms had to carry. The increased minimum wage, the reduction of working time (the 39-hour week, the fifth week of paid vacation), earlier retirement, higher Social Security contributions, and the increase in the *taxe professionnelle* were estimated to cost over 90 billion francs yearly, although the government came up with a substantially lower figure. In contrast, additional aids to business were put by the CNPF at a mere 11 billion francs.[295] Given the dismal state of the French economy, the employers' organization predicted a sudden increase of bankruptcies, a further fall in investment, and the continued rise of unemployment unless measures were taken to encourage private initiative anew.[296]

In his meetings with Prime Minister Mauroy and President Mitterrand, Yvon Gattaz stressed the urgent need for some reduction in the financial burdens on business, especially as the increase in these burdens coincided with a decrease abroad and thus made French firms even less competitive. Economics Minister Delors was himself in favor of making concessions to business, though he questioned the calculations put forward by the CNPF. When he called for a pause in reforms in December of 1981, however, this caused considerable controversy among the Socialist leadership.

It was clear that Mitterrand's and Mauroy's thinking was shaped by Leon Blum's experience; important concessions to business before any of the major social reforms had been enacted carried with it the danger of alienating the voters that had brought the Left to power. Concessions could also make business (and the Right) even less yielding and willing to accommodate.[297] But after several months of negotiations and the decreeing of several social reforms, a compromise was reached, soon termed the *pause Mauroy* described above. Business expressed its satisfaction and saw the *pause* as evidence that the government finally recognized the real problems of the business world.[298] Gattaz in turn promised that French business would do its best to help the government achieve its policy goals. Soon after the *pause*, the CNPF came up with a program to strengthen cooperation among French business firms to reduce imports, encourage research and development, and achieve other governmental goals.[299] When in September 1982 the government postponed the application of the wealth tax to business firms, the CNPF expressed great satisfaction.

To be sure, new problems surfaced once the question of financial charges was settled. Many employers were upset by the *rapport Auroux* and the legislation derived from it. They predicted that irreparable damage would be done to business efficiency by the attempts to introduce democracy to the workplace and by the privileged place granted to labor unions.[300] But there was no longer the feeling that the government was ignorant of all business realities. After a year of Socialist government, French business seemed prepared to play its role with a certain amount of loyalty; sabotage no longer seemed a serious alternative.

After Giscard's defeat, mutually hostile feelings dominated the leadership of the two parties of the Right. The loss of the presidency of the Republic was followed by another, perhaps even more demoralizing, setback, in the elections for the National Assembly. The catastrophe was particularly marked for the Giscardiens' UDF, which received only 19.20 percent of the vote and saw the number of its deputies fall from 120 to 64.[301] Since then, the elements united by Giscard as part of his presidential majority turned in different directions as Giscard withdrew from the political scene; he did not come out of hiding again until early 1982.

One of the three groups that form the UDF, the *Centre des démocrates sociaux* (CDS), seemed eager to emancipate itself from Giscard's leadership. Some of the Radicals considered an alliance with Chirac's RPR.[302] As no clear leader emerged to take the lead, the UDF was becoming the victim of centrifugal forces. It is probably this fact that decided Giscard to make a relatively early political comeback, despite considerable doubts about his leadership in the ranks of his own party. In April 1982, he became a member of the party's executive bureau; in June, he was acclaimed again at the congress of the Republican Party.[303] However, the UDF had done little thinking about a new program, and had not developed a coherent political strategy. There was a general feeling that a renewed rivalry with Chirac could only lead to another disaster, but there was also the recognition that the party needed a viable presidential candidate if it wanted to play a major role in French politics. Giscard seemed well on the way to persuade a reluctant party that he was in fact just such a candidate.

It was partly due to this vacuum that the Gaullists, or

rather the RPR under Chirac, fared somewhat better in their first year in opposition. By a wide margin Chirac had lost his gamble to make it to the second round of the presidential election. In the subsequent National Assembly elections the RPR gathered only 20.80 percent of the vote, reducing the number of its deputies from 155 to 88 despite the fact that Chirac had quickly organized a rightist coalition after Giscard's defeat.[304] The UDF deputies at that point panicked, and Chirac prevailed with his proposal to form an electoral coalition (the Union for a New Majority—UNM) for the first round—a coalition that gave a better place to the candidates of the RPR.[305] From then on, Chirac continued to try to establish himself as the only viable leader of the Right, an enterprise in which he was helped by the UDF's divisions. More than ever, the RPR now became the party of Chirac. In his effort to renovate it, Chirac dropped all references to de Gaulle and Pompidou; the old Gaullist leaders (including Debré) are no longer to play major roles. This development was confirmed at the Toulouse party congress in early 1982. The party is also to be given a new doctrine.[306]

In the meantime, the RPR (and to some extent the Right generally) had shown a certain trend toward extremism, at least verbally. Some of its members claim that the 1981 elections were really based on a misunderstanding; others portray the Socialist-Communist coalition as a first step toward totalitarianism.[307] Especially after the regional elections, which the Right won somewhat to its own surprise, several rightists questioned the legitimacy of the Socialist government and even of the president of the Republic. Michel Debré declared that the Socialist-Communist government used to be *legitimate,* but that now it was only the *legal* government of France.[308] Alain Peyrefitte spoke in similar terms and Claude Labbé, a prominent leader of the RPR, called publicly for the resignation of both Mitterrand and Mauroy.

Chirac at first disapproved of these statements, but he

was suspected of playing a double game.[309] In late summer 1982, Chirac changed his stand and announced that the Socialist government would collapse very soon and that early elections would be necessary.[310] In the National Assembly, the Gaullists practiced systematic obstruction, inviting special legislative procedures which they could then denounce as authoritarian.[311] The UDF was considerably more moderate in its opposition; both Giscard and Barre occasionally stated their approval of certain aspects of Socialist policy.[312]

The difference between the two parties illustrated a problem that the Right did not confront in its first year in opposition. To return to power at the national level, a measure of agreement on a program will be necessary, especially for the elections to the National Assembly—in 1986. Neither opposition party has made much progress on this account, however. It is true that time is not terribly pressing, unless one assumes, as leaders in both parties have occasionally claimed, that the Socialist government will soon go down in disgrace.

But assuming that a leadership struggle between Chirac and Giscard can be avoided, will the two major opposition parties be able to agree on a common program? This problem did not present itself in the by-elections of January 1982, nor in the regional elections two months later; the common attacks on the Socialist reforms provided an easy substitute. The victory of the Right in these elections came as a surprise, and one would probably do well not to overestimate its importance.[313] It seems extremely unlikely that they amounted to a repudiation of Socialist policies. Public opinion polls in any case showed that, on the level of national politics, the government still enjoyed strong majority support throughout the country. This situation changed only during the summer of 1982 when, after a few months of the wage and price freeze, negative opinions of the government outweighed the positive ones.[314]

Political and Economic Viability

Even a positive public opinion rating would of course not guarantee the political future of the government and its policies; electoral and economic success will also be necessary. And even if the Socialist Party should continue to progress with the electorate, the weakness of its allies, particularly of the Communists, may represent an increasingly serious problem as shown in the regional elections of March 1982.[315] As a result, several prominent Socialist leaders have gone on record to proclaim the need for the Socialist Party to broaden its appeal and recruit from among the political center. One of these statements came from Michel Rocard, who would like to see the "modernist" bourgeoisie included in the leftist coalition. The other (and more surprising) statement came from Jean-Pierre Chevènement, once the leader of the pro-Communist CERES; he wanted to see the party make an effort to include artisans, small businessmen, farmers, and similar groups.[316] Undoubtedly, either course will mean a change in policy. The CGT's position, often favored by Mitterrand, is likely to suffer. But then the first year of Socialist rule has shown that economic rigor was not necessarily an unpopular position. Rocard, Delors, and Maire, all advocates of a more stringent policy, did not suffer any setbacks with public opinion for the stand they took. The regional elections may have conveyed a similar message.[317]

Such an evolution—toward greater economic austerity—seemed to be required in any case by the evolution of the French economy. The reflation of fall 1981 had had a mild stimulative effect, but stagnation returned in the spring of 1982. France's major problems, however, were international in nature; they derived from the fact that the evolution of the economy in France went in an opposite direction from that of most of its trading partners.[318] This aggravated the inflation differential between France and its international economic environment and led to the dramatic import surge of April 1982. In other words, the external constraints that rein in the French economy now came to be felt with much greater force and threatened to undermine Socialist economic policy. By the autumn of 1982, the external deficit seemed likely to reach 100 billion francs for the current year, up from about 60 billion a year earlier. At the same time, another devaluation of the franc hardly seemed acceptable politically. The external constraints came to be felt with an unprecedented force.

It is of course these external constraints that the Socialists are trying to lift. Nationalization, the reconquest of domestic markets, the program for energy savings, and the project of a European social space (a movement of coordinated social reforms throughout the European Community) all go in this direction. France's major trading partners must have mixed feelings about such policies. In any case, most of these programs will not have a positive impact before the mid-1980s, and there is no guarantee that they will have one by that time. It will be politically difficult to maintain public support for a policy that will impose its share of pain, can only show its strength over the long run, and can offer little certainty of success in the end. There are definite parallels with the policy of the preceding government, but this should not obscure the important differences in method between the approach of Raymond Barre and that of François Mitterrand.

Notes

1. But the economic crisis of the 1970s has changed many things. Britain was long famous for its "stop-go" policies, but Prime Minister Margaret Thatcher seems to have put the British economy quite clearly in "reverse."
2. David P. Calleo and Benjamin M. Rowland, *America and the World Political Economy* (Bloomington: Indiana University Press, 1973), pp. 88-93.
3. This was the time of the optimistic predictions made by the Hudson Institute Paris. See Edmund O. Stillman, et al., *L'envol de la France dans les années 80* (Paris: Hachette, 1973); Paul Dubois, "La rupture de 1974," *Economie et statistique* (August 1980), p. 18.
4. *Eurostat Review, 1970-1979* (Brussels: October 1980), p. 138; Dubois, "La rupture de 1974," p. 16.
5. Organization for Economic Cooperation and Development (OECD), *Main Economic Indicators* (Paris: OECD, August 1981), pp. 46, 47.
6. OECD, *OECD Economic Surveys: France* (Paris: OECD, January 1982), p. 16.
7. Pierre Muller and Philippe Tassi, "1979: année favorable pour les entreprises industrielles," *Economie et statistique* (February 1981), pp. 9,10,12; *Le Monde,* March 10, 1981, pp. 22,

24; Jacky Fayolle, "Le comportement d'investissement depuis 1974," *Economie et statistique* (November 1980), p. 34; *Bulletin du Crédit National* (first trimester 1981), p. 26.

8. *Eurostat Review, 1970-1979,* p. 148. From 1971 to 1973, Germany, Britain, the United States, and Japan all had small increases in real wages. Among the major industrial countries, only Italy had rates comparable to France.

9. Pierre Cohen-Tanugi and Christian Morrisson, *Salaires intérêts profits dans l'industrie française, 1968-1976* (Paris: Presses de la FNSP, 1979), pp. 257-263.

10. Ibid., p. 146; Yves Meffredi, "Quelle stratégie économique à moyen terme?" *Projet* (March 1978), pp. 327-336.

11. C. Phéline, "répartition primaire des revenus et rentabilité du capital (1954-1973), *Statistiques et études financières,* no. 19 (1975), p. 3; Also see Cohen-Tanugi and Morrisson, *Salaires intérêts profits,* p. 39 (citing C. Phéline), pp. 219-220.

12. OCED, *Main Economic Indicators* (August 1981).

13. OCED *Economic Surveys: France,* 1982.

14. *Bulletin du Crédit National,* first trimester, 1981.

15. Muller and Tassi, "1979: année favorable." *Le Monde,* March 10, pp. 22, 24.

16. Muller and Tassi, "1979; année favorable," p. 10.

17. OCED, *Main Economic Indicators:* J. G. Mérigot, "Le Plan Barre," *Défense nationale* (November 1976), pp. 99-109.

18. According to Arthur Conte, "Giscard m'a dit," *Paris-Match* (March 6, 1981), p. 3841, excerpting passages from Conte, *L'homme Giscard* (Paris: Plon, 1981).

19. Some of the leading French economic journalists pointed that out from the very beginning. See Roger Priouret, "Barre, ce qui manque," *L'Express,* October 4, 1976; Jean Boissonnat, "Le véritable objectif du plan Barre," *L'Expansion* (October 1976); also Philippe Lefournier, "Plan Barre: un succès inavouable," *L'Expansion* (October 1977).

20. C. Phéline, "répartition primaire."

21. Cohen-Tanugi and Morrisson, *Salaires intérêts profits,* p. 35.

22. Muller and Tassi, "1979: année favorable," p. 10.

98   The Politics of Economic Policy

23. Interview with Raymond Barre, *L'Expansion* (September 1978), p. 163.

24. This corresponds to the "Little Germany" option described by David Calleo, *The German Problem Reconsidered* (New York: Cambridge University Press, 1978), pp. 88-90.

25. Roger Priouret, "Le feu de 'bois mort' de Raymond Barre," *Le Nouvel Observateur*, April 24, 1978; and Bruno Dethomas, "Le 'vrai' plan Barre," *Le Monde*, July 13, 1979.

26. Lefournier, "Plan Barre," p. 110.

27. *Programme de Blois* (Paris: Fayard, 1978), pp. 39-40. For the results, see *Le Monde*, March 10, 1981, p. 22.

28. *European Economy*, no. 8 (March 1981), p. 63.

29. Herbert Rowen in the *International Herald Tribune*, October 2, 1978; Rolf E. Wubbels, "The French Economic Miracle: What a Difference Leadership Makes," *Financial Analysts Journal* (July-August 1978), pp. 23-27; Muller and Tassi, "1979: année favorable," pp. 9, 10, 12.

30. Muller and Tassi, "1979: année favorable," pp. 9, 10, 12.

31. Paul Lewis in the *International Herald Tribune*, September 14, 1978; and Alain Vernholes in *Le Monde*, May 15, 1981.

32. This was a constant concern to the government, and a threatening prediction used by the opposition. See, for example, Barre, cited by Alain Rollat in *Le Monde*, January 10, 1981.

33. Interview with Barre, *L'Expansion* (September 1978), pp. 154-163; and Marc Clairvois, "Le frisson keynésien de Barre," *L'Expansion* (September 7, 1979), pp. 28-29.

34. Interview with *L'Expansion* (September 1978), p. 159.

35. Jean Boissonnat, "Raymond Barre m'a dit . . .," *L'Expansion* (April 1977), p. 30.

36. Interview with *L'Expansion* (September 1978); similarly Giscard d'Estaing in a speech on September 20, 1978; *Le Monde*, September 22, 1978.

37. "How the Barre plan is making its mark," *Financial Times*, January 11, 1980.

38. "Premier ministre des temps difficiles," *Le Monde*, September 5, 1979.

39. The projections are listed in detail in *Bilan économique et social, 1979* (Supplément aux Dossiers et Documents du Monde,

January 1980), pp. 50-51. For the government's reactions, see Jean Boissonnat, "La 'sagesse' de Barre," *La Croix*, January 13-14, 1980; Hobart Rowen, "The success of France Inc.," *International Herald Tribune*, May 15, 1980; and Henry Busséry, "La vérité est bonne à dire," *Projet* (September-October 1980, pp. 904-907.

40. Thus, just before the elections, Jean-Pierre Fourcade (one of the leaders of the UDF): "L'économie et l'emploi," *Le Monde*, April 16, 1981. Interestingly, he does not once mention Barre's name.

41. Starting in 1977, there were three National Employment Pacts that subsidized employment in a variety of ways, mostly by facilitating job training or by exempting employers from social contributions. The number of beneficiaries was 579 thousand in 1977-1978 (first Pact), 313 thousand in 1978-1979, 455 thousand in 1979-1980 and a planned 534 thousand for 1980-1981. The employers did not need to commit themselves to maintain the beneficiaries in their jobs once the subsidies were terminated and often did not do so. (Most of the employers taking advantage of this formula were small businessmen and artisans.) As to the premiums for immigrant workers who left France (instituted in May 1977), only 23 thousand persons took advantage of it by the end of 1978. Olivier Marchand and Jean-Pierre Revoil, "Emploi et chômage: bilan fin 1980," *Economie et statistique* (February 1981), pp. 40-42.

42. For example, Maurice Blin, a centrist senator and budget rapporteur: "Mon inquiétude, le refus du futur...," *La Croix*, October 10, 1979. For the previous practice and tradition, see Andrew Shonfield, *Modern Capitalism* (New York: Oxford University Press, 1969), pp. 134-140. Much of this apparatus was still in place in the 1970s.

43. "Premier ministre des temps difficiles," *Le Monde*, September 5, 1979; and Pierre Locardel in *Les Echos*, February 20, 1980.

44. Colette Ysmal, "Nature et réalité de l'affrontement Giscard-Chirac," *Politique aujourd'hui*, nos. 3-4 (1978), p. 14. Giscard expressed this concern already in 1972; see his contributions in *Economie et société humaine* (Paris: Denoël, 1972).

45. Michael Kreile, "West Germany: The Dynamics of Ex-

pansion," in Peter J. Katzenstein, ed., *Between Power and Plenty* (Madison: University of Wisconsin Press, 1978), pp. 208-217.

46. Alain Rollat, "M. Barre affirme que le budget de 1981 ne sera pas inspiré par des 'considérations électoralistes,'" *Le Monde*, July 9, 1980; and Dominique Audibert, "Des lendemains qui divergent," *Le Point*, November 24, 1980. See also Jacques Lecaillon, "Entrons-nous dans un nouveau cycle électoral?," *La Croix*, July 30, 1980; Jean-Gabriel Fredet, "La relance économique au secours du 'bon choix,'" *Le Matin*, April 8, 1980; and Bernard Hartemann, "L'économie 'électorale' de 1981," *La vie française*, June 9, 1980.

47. The short-term growth of the indices of production for all industry (excluding building) showed a negative evolution for every one of the 12 months preceding the presidential election. The worst figures were in the two months preceding the election; the trend changed direction in June. See *Industrial Short-Term Trends* (Eurostat), June 1981, Table II, and October 1981, Table 2. The figures are as follows:

1980

May	June	July	Aug.	Sept.	Oct.	Nov.	Dec.
−0.4	−1.4	−2.2	−1.2	−1.3	−1.8	−3.2	−1.5

1981

Jan.	Feb.	Mar.	Apr.	May	June	July	Aug.
−1.9	−1.9	−4.5	−3.2	−1.5	+0.1	+0.8	+1.1

48. For his plan, see *Le Figaro*, March 28-29, 1981 and March 31, 1981.

49. Muller and Tassi, "1979: année favorable," p. 9, 10, 12.

50. *Bulletin du Crédit National*, first trimester, 1981.

51. Fayolle, "La Comportement d'investissement," p. 33.

52. Ibid., p. 34.

53. For the comparison with the United States and Japan, see *Eurostat Review, 1970-1979* (Luxemburg: European Communities, 1981), p. 148.

54. Jean-Michel Lamy, "Le redressement de l'économie,"

Les Echos, August 24, 1979; Gilbert Mathieu, "Pourquoi avoir échoué," *Le Monde,* August 22, 1979; *Le Monde,* May 21, 1981, p. 10.

55. Muller and Tassi, "1979: année favorable," p. 10.
56. At the end of 1980, unemployment in Germany was 4 percent, compared with approximately 6.3 percent in France. *Bilan économique et social* (Paris: *Le Monde,* January 1981), p. 17. For the evolution of growth rates in the European Community, see *Industrial Short-Term Trends* (Luxemburg: Eurostat, October, 1981).
57. The Gaullist RPR gathered 22.62 percent of the vote, the highest percentage, the Communist Party the lowest percentage with 20.55 percent. René Rémond, "Les élections législatives," *Paradoxes* (April–May 1978), pp. 25–32.
58. Interview with Jean Lecanuet, *Les Echos,* September 12, 1978; Jean-Pierre Fourcade, "Dynamisme et solidarité," *L'Express,* March 24, 1979; and André Diligent, "Le bilan," *Démocratie moderne,* September 6, 1979.
59. Articles by Albin Chalandon, *Le Monde,* October 2, 1979; and by Olivier Guichard, *Le Monde,* October 30, 1979.
60. Articles by André Passeron in the *Guardian* (weekly) (December 8, 1979), p. 11, and December 16, 1979, p. 11.
61. Alain Peyrefitte, *Le Mal français* (Paris: Plon, 1976), pp. 404 and 440–450.
62. *Propositions pour la France* (Paris: Stock, 1977), pp. 173–176, 185–187, 194–195; Colette Ysmal, "Nature et réalité de l'affrontement Giscard-Chirac," *Politique aujourd'hui,* nos. 3–4 (1978), pp. 11–23; Pierre Dabeziès, "Gaullisme et giscardisme," *Pouvoirs,* no. 9 (1979), pp. 27–36; and "Déclaration politique du groupe parlementaire UDF, commentée par le RPR," ibid., pp. 49–52.
63. *Propositions pour la France,* pp. 59–61, 140–141, 165, and 230; Pierre Charpy, *Lettre de la Nation,* July 13, 1979; Michel Debré, *Le Figaro,* September 18, 1979; Jacques Chirac, *Le Monde,* March 29–30, 1980. These are but a few examples; the theme is constant.
64. *Propositions pour la France,* pp. 184–189; Philippe Dechartre, "L'emploi: vouloir la relance," *Le Matin* (September

1978); Chirac, "Oui, la relance est possible," *Le Nouvel Observateur,* May 14, 1979; and Chirac, *Le Monde,* March 5, 1979 and May 14, 1979.

65. *Propositions pour la France,* p. 219; and Chirac, *Le Monde,* April 15, 1980.

66. Michel Garibal, "Le rapport Méo," *Journal des Finances,* September 27, 1979.

67. *Propositions pour la France,* pp. 184-189; Debré, interview in *Les Echos,* September 6, 1978.

68. Chirac, interview in *Le Nouvel Observateur,* May 14, 1979.

69. Jean Méo in *Forum International,* October 4, 1979 and December 21, 1979, and in *Le Monde,* June 27, 1980.

70. Philippe Bauchard, *L'Expansion* (November 9-22, 1979); Gilbert Mathieu, *Le Monde,* February 14, 1980; Pierre Locardel, *Les Echos,* February 13, 1980.

71. *Le Monde,* April 15, 1980.

72. Debré, "Un grand dessein pour la France?" *Bulletin ACADI* (January-February 1978), pp. 34-58; and Debré in *Forum International,* August 29, 1979. Debré in *Le Figaro,* June 12, 1978, and in *Le Monde,* February 14, 1979; also Chirac, interview in *Paradoxes* (February 1975), pp. 58-59.

73. Chirac, *Le Nouvel Observateur,* May 14, 1979; discussed by Gilbert Mathieu in *Le Monde,* April 16, 1980; Debré, *Forum International,* August 29, 1979; and *L'Expansion* (December 21, 1979).

74. *Propositions pour la France,* pp. 177-178.

75. Méo, "On ne peut promener le pays de tunnel en tunnel," *Forum International,* October 4, 1979; also Chirac, interview in *L'Expansion,* November 9-22, 1979; Méo, *Le Monde,* June 27, 1980.

76. Chirac, "La participation est la dernière chance de la liberté," *Paradoxes* (October-November 1977), pp. 75-79; Debré, "Un grand dessein pour la France?" *Bulletin ACADI* (January-February 1978), pp. 44-45; *Propositions pour la France,* p. 169; Chirac, *Le Monde,* April 15, 1980.

77. Chirac, interview in *Paradoxes* (February 1975), p. 57.

78. *Propositions pour la France,* p. 181; Chirac in *Le Nouvel Observateur,* November 9, 1979.

79. Méo, *Forum International*, October 4, 1979; and Chirac, *L'Expansion* (November 9-22, 1979). (He talked then of 4-5 percent.)
80. *Le Nouvel Obervateur*, April 28, 1981, p. 21; *Le Monde*, (weekly edition) January 7, 1982, p. 4.
81. J. R. Frears, *Political Parties and Elections in the French Fifth Republic* (London: C. Hurst, 1977), pp. 24-25; Georges Lavau, "The Effect of Twenty Years of Gaullism on the Parties of the Left," in William G. Andrews and Stanley Hoffmann, eds., *The Fifth Republic at Twenty* (Albany: SUNY Press, 1981), pp. 161-162.
82. *Manifeste de Champigny*, published in *Cahiers du Communisme* (January 1969). Roger Priouret, *Les Français mystifiés* (Paris: Grasset, 1973), pp. 166-175 and 201-225.
83. In particular, he was in charge then of nationalizations. Thierry Pfister, "Le faux-pas de Jean-Pierre Chevènement," *Le Nouvel Observateur*, October 15, 1979.
84. Edmond Maire and Jacques Julliard, "La C.F.D.T. aujourd'hui," (Paris: Le Seuil, 1975), pp. 164-168; *Manifeste du P.S.U.* (Paris: Téma, 1972), pp. 34-37 and 88-89. At that time Rocard was still the leader of the PSU.
85. "Mitterrand répond à Giscard," *L'Unité*, July 11-17, 1975; Guy Perrimond, "Quelle relance?" *L'Unité*, September 5-11, 1975.
86. Jean Boissonnat, "Les deux stratégies," *L'Expansion* (July-August 1977).
87. Pierre Mauroy, "Les deux faces du plan Barre," *Revue politique et parlementaire* (September-October 1976), pp. 6-10; Jacques Gallus, "A quoi sert le plan Barre," *Faire* (October 1976), pp. 6-8.
88. Contributions by Mitterrand, Rocard, Attali and Fuchs in *Faire*, December 1976. Kathleen Evin and Roland Cayrol, "Comment contrôler l'union," *Projet* (January 1978), pp. 64-74.
89. Michel Rocard, "La gauche et les pouvoirs," *Bulletin ACADI* (January-February 1978), pp. 9-10; and Ivan Levai, "Michel Rocard fait le point," *Paradoxes*, (February-March 1978), pp. 20-23; also Yves Rocaute, *Le PCF et les sommets de l'Etat* (Paris: PUF, 1981), excerpted in *Le Point*, January 18, 1981, pp. 42-43.
90. Rocard, "La gauche et les pouvoirs," pp. 10-12; Ro-

card, "Nationaliser: oui mais comment?" in Michel Rocard, *Parler vrai* (Paris: Le Seuil, 1979), pp. 143-149.

91. *Le Nouvel Observateur*, November 27, 1978, p. 47; December 4, 1978, pp. 62-63; December 18, 1978, pp. 44 and 45; January 8, 1979, pp. 28-29; April 14, 1979, pp. 32-35. Hugues Portelli, "Guerre de succession au PS," *Projet* (June 1979), pp. 739-742; *Le Nouvel Observateur*, June 25, 1979, pp. 32-33.

92. Jean-Marie Colombani, in *Le Monde*, March 15, 1980.

93. Attack by Laurent Fabius: George Mamy in *Le Nouvel Observateur*, April 14, 1979, pp. 33-35; by Jean-Pierre Chevènement: Thierry Pfister, *Le Nouvel Observateur*, October 15, 1979. In a sample survey, 57 percent of the category "liberal professions, executives and businessmen" had a good opinion of Rocard (bad opinion: 25 percent); for Mitterrand, the figures were 45 percent (good opinion) and 43 percent (bad opinion). *Sondages*, nos. 2 and 3, 1978, p. 74.

94. Gilbert Mathieu in *Le Monde*, July 10, 1979.

95. The program as presented before the economic journalists is discussed in *Le Monde*, June 23, and July 10, 1979; it is presented in greater detail in *L'Unité*, June 29, 1979.

96. Pierre Locardel in *Les Echos*, June 22, 1979.

97. Kathleen Evin in *Le Nouvel Observateur*, January 14, 1980.

98. *Le Nouvel Observateur*, April 9, 1979, p. 46; *L'Expansion* (September 21, 1979), p. 91; *Le Monde*, April 1, 1980, pp. 1 and 8; *Le Point*, November 17, 1980, p. 78.

99. *Le Point*, November 17 and December 1, 1980.

100. Such a strategy was already proposed in 1979 by Jean-Pierre Cot (*Le Nouvel Observateur*, January 8, 1979, pp. 28-29), and Rocard (Hugues Portelli, "La guerre de succession au PS," *Projet*, June 1979, pp. 739-742). Mitterrand seems to have adopted that view in 1980 (Jean-Marie Colombani in *Le Monde*, March 11, 1980, p. 11; Jean Boissonnat, *L'Expansion*, March 7, 1980, pp. 53-57).

101. *L'Express*, April 29, 1974, p. 23.

102. A large part of *Propositions pour la France* is devoted to this enterprise. Much of the same criticism was repeated (with less justification) in 1981 (see for example Jean Lecanuet in *Le*

Monde, April 18, 1981) and by Giscard himself after the first round. See Maurice Duverger, "L'épouvantail," *Le Monde* (weekly edition), April 23, 1981, p. 1.

103. Jean Boissonnat, "Les deux stratégies," *L'Expansion* (July-August 1977); Pierre Locardel, *Les Echos,* June 22, 1979.

104. *Le Monde,* April 9, 1981, p. 12.

105. *IFOP Report* AV.01-F.8.468 (January 1977).

106. For a discussion of the public sector, see George Perrineau, "L'ampleur actuelle du champ des nationalisations," *Revue politique et parlementaire* (July 1981), pp. 56-64.

107. Antoine Laurent, *Le Monde,* May 9, 1981. (It must be added that by this time Chirac had discovered supply-side economics and was quite far from his 1975-1976 policy.) Interestingly, already in 1979 Gilles Martinet (close to Rocard) spoke a language similar to that of Chirac: "economic warfare," and investments as "armaments." Gilles Martinet, "Pour une vraie politique de salut public," *Faire* (September 1979), pp. 3-6.

108. *Le Nouvel Observateur,* April 28, 1981, p. 21; *Le Monde,* (weekly edition) January 7, 1982, p. 4.

109. Kathleen Evin and Roland Cayrol, "Comment contrôler l'union?" *Projet* (January 1978), pp. 64-74.

110. Evin and Cayrol, "Comment contrôler l'union?" Hugues Portelli, "Que se passe-t-il au parti socialiste?" *Projet* (January 1978), pp. 45-63; J. C. Simmons, "The French Communist Party in 1978: Conjugating the Future Imperfect," *Parliamentary Affairs,* 32:1 (Winter 1979), pp. 79-91.

111. Evin and Cayrol, "Comment contrôler l'union?" pp. 69-73; Colette Ysmal, "Parti Communiste: Les raisons d'un durcissement," *Projet* (January 1978), pp. 44-54. According to Rocard, Charles Fiterman of the PCF had already accepted the Socialist refusal to nationalize the subsidiaries when he counted up the cost of the nationalizations in an interview with *Les Echos,* in February 1977; Rocard, *Parler vrai,* p. 148.

112. Claude Harmel, "Ce que les Communistes ont voulu," *Est et Ouest,* March 15-31, 1978, pp. 112-115. In 1980 the Socialist leaders were not taken aback by this attitude.

113. Editorial "Remèdes à la sinistrose," *L'Humanité,* March 1, 1980.

114. *Le Point,* October 6 and 20, 1980.

115. Jean-Pierre Gaudard, "Quelle politique économique et sociale pour la France?" *Cahiers du communisme* (November 1977), pp. 14-23.

116. Marc Bormann, "Le démantèlement du potential industriel national," *Cahirs du communisme* (November 1976, pp. 23-30; Jean-Louis Gombeaud, "Gagner?" *France Nouvelle,* October 1978; and Jean-Louis Gombeaud, "Appauvrir la France," *France Nouvelle,* August 4, 1979.

117. Bernard Marx et al., "Avec les Communistes les moyens du changement," *Economie et politique* (February 1978), pp. 54-78; and Colette Ysmal,"Parti Communiste: les raisons d'un durcissement," *Projet* (January 1978), pp. 44-54.

118. Juliette Petit, "Sidérurgie: Le P.S. contre la nationalisation," ibid., pp. 49-51; Claude Gauche-Cazalis, "Une sidérurgie d'un type nouveau," *Economie et politique* (April 1979), pp. 60-66.

119. Mireille Bertrand, "Offensive antisociale et antinationale—une même strategie: celle du déclin," *Cahiers du communisme* (February 1979), pp. 4-12; Philippe Herzog in *L'Express,* March 31, 1979, and in *Le Monde,* August 23, 1979.

120. Marchais in *Le Monde,* February 27, 1981.

121. On the other hand, it seems that the party gave also secret instructions to militants to help defeat Mitterrand, see Patrick Jarreau in *Le Monde,* January 9 and 11, 1982.

122. "Investissements: Remonter la pente," *CNPF Patronat* (September 1976), pp. 3-7.

123. Marc Clairvois, "Ceyrac vire à gauche," *L'Expansion* (November 1977), p. 39.

124. Interview with François Ceyrac, *Usine Nouvelle* (December 1977), pp. 48-50; and Jacques Ferry, "Les impératifs de la croissance," *CNPF Patronat* (February 1978), pp. 11ff.

125. François-Henri de Virieu, "Le patronat prépare 1978," *Faire* (November 1976), pp. 2-6.

126. "Le plan Barre," *CNPF Patronat* (October 1976), pp. 6-8.

127. "Une croissance forte est necessaire," *Notes et Arguments* (Paris: CNPF May 1976).

128. "Investissements: remonter la pente," *CNPF Patronat* (September 1976), pp. 3-7.
129. Jacques Ferry, "Une nouvelle politique pour l'industrie," *CNPF Patronat* (February 1977), pp. 19-28.
130. Interview with François Ceyrac, *Usine Nouvelle* (December 1977), p. 49. There is considerable truth to this; see the discussion of the Socialists' policy on unemployment later on.
131. Jacques Ferry, "Les impératifs de la croissance," *CNPF Patronat* (February 1978), pp. 15 and 18.
132. Pierre Locardel in *Les Echos*, October 3, 1979.
133. Ibid., and Michel Garibal in *Journal des Finances*, September 27, 1979.
134. André Giraud, interview with *Le Monde*, September 22, 1979.
135. Interview with Alain Chevalier, vice president of the CNPF; *La Croix*, October 19, 1979.
136. J. van den Esch in *L'Aurore*, January 9, 1980.
137. Guy de Carmoy, "Industrie française et industrie allemande: performances et stratégies," *Politique internationale*, no. 6 (Winter 1979-1980), pp. 137-138.
138. Survey by SOFRES: *L'Expansion*, April 17, 1981, pp. 93-95.
139. Georges Lavau, "The Effect of Twenty Years of Gaullism on the Parties of the Left," in William G. Andrews and Stanley Hoffman, eds., *The Fifth Republic at Twenty* (Albany: SUNY Press, 1981), p. 161; and George Ross, "Gaullism and Organized Labor—Two Decades of Failure?" ibid., pp. 336-337.
140. The parties of the Left entered a decline with the 1968 elections; the labor unions, on the other hand, progressed during this time. Jean Bunel, "L'action syndicale; crise et recentrage," *Economie et Humanisme* (January-February 1979), pp. 4-11.
141. "Engagées ou non, la plupart des organisations prônent la prudence et le réalisme," *Le Monde*, May 9, 1981.
142. Emile Favard, "Révisions déchirantes dans les syndicats," *L'Expansion* (December 1977), pp. 34-35.
143. Jean Bunel, "L'action syndicale"; and Pierre Rosonvallon, "Le syndicalisme au tournant," *Projet* (November 1978), pp. 1033-1059.

144. Claude-François Jullien and Lucien Rioux, "Les syndicats en ordre dispersé," *Le Nouvel Observateur*, January 15, 1979, pp. 35-36; and *Les Echos*, January 18, 1979.
145. Interview with Edmond Maire, *Le Nouvel Observateur*, February 19, 1979, pp. 28-30.
146. Jullien and Rioux, "Les syndicats en ordre dispersé,"
147. Ibid.
148. Dominique Pouchin, "Le syndicalisme en crise," *Le Monde*, March 5, 1980. The connection between the strength of French labor unions and the political fortunes of the Left has manifested itself several times during this century; see Stanley Rothman, Howard Scarrow, and Martin Schain, *European Society and Politics* (St. Paul: West, 1976), p. 73.
149. OECD, *Main Economic Indicators, 1960-1979* (Pans: OECD, 1980), p. 293; *Le Monde* (weekly edition), February 12, 1981, p. 4.
150. Pouchin, "Syndicalisme en crise," *Le Monde*, March 6 and 7, 1980; "L'Aveu," *CNPF Patronat* (December 1978), pp. 31-35; and Jean Bonis, "Nouveaux modes d'action managériales et syndicats," *Economie et humanisme* (May-June 1981), pp. 31-39.
151. "Engagées ou non, la plupart des organisations syndicales...," *Le Monde*, May 9, 1981; J.-M. Quatrepoint, "Les industriels dans l'expectative," *Le Monde*, May 16, 1981. For the political attitudes and sympathies of union members in April 1981, see *Le Nouvel Observateur*, April 13, 1981, pp. 26-27.
152. See Andrews and Hoffmann, eds., *The Fifth Republic at Twenty*, pp. 19 and 228-229.
153. For comparisons with earlier presidents and prime ministers, see the IFOP data cited in *Le Point*, June 24, 1981, p. 39. De Gaulle had said of Giscard: *"Son problème à lui, c'est le peuple"* (His problem is—the people). Cited by J. Boissonnat in *L'Expansion* (April 17, 1981).
154. *Sondages*, 1978, nos. 2 and 3, pp. 43, 48; SOFRES, *L'Expansion* (September 21, 1979), pp. 96 and 97.
155. *Sondages*, 1976, nos. 3 and 4, p. 78; 1978, nos. 2 and 3, pp. 44, 49, 78; *IFOP Report*, AV.01-F.8.468 (January 1977).
156. *Le Monde*, May 15, 1981, p. 10.

157. Alain Rollat in *Le Monde,* January 18, 1981. Surveys proved inaccurate when they predicted a leftist victory in 1978. It is also true that survey results have on occasion been manipulated, see *Le Nouvel Observateur,* January 8, 1979, pp. 26-27.

158. *Le Figaro,* March 29 and 31, 1981, April 9, 1981; R. Priouret in *Le Nouvel Observateur,* April 6, 1981; and E. Favard and A. Murcier in *L'Expansion* (April 3, 1981).

159. Giscard as finance minister had applied an austerity plan before 1965; he was also asked to campaign for de Gaulle in the 1965 elections, which he did—only to be dropped right afterwards.

160. R. Priouret in *Le Nouvel Observateur,* March 9, 1981; Philippe Lefournier in *L'Expansion* (May 1, 1981).

161. Roland Cayrol, "Le godillot et le commissaire politique." *Projet* (January 1982), pp. 32-41.

162. In the previous Assembly, the Socialists had held 117 seats. *Le Monde* (weekly edition), January 7, 1982.

163. Mitterrand press conference of June 9, 1982; see *Le Monde,* June 11, 1982. Mitterrand cited the following figures for investment in the nationalized industries: 10 billion francs in 1979; 11.7 billion in 1980; 12.8 billion in 1981; 16.3 billion in 1982; and about 25 billion in 1983.

164. *Le Monde,* June 15, 1982.

165. *Le Monde,* September 3, 1982.

166. *Le Monde,* September 17, 1982.

167. Alain Boublil, *Le socialisme industriel* (Paris: Presses universitaires de France, 1977).

168. Ibid., pp. 15-17. He adds that it might work in the United States, where foreign trade plays a much more modest role (p. 62).

169. Ibid., pp. 38-46.

170. Ibid., p. 62.

171. Ibid., pp. 72-82.

172. Ibid., pp. 259-260.

173. Ibid., pp. 51-52.

174. The infant industries argument holds that tariff protection is appropriate as long as it is temporary and designed to help industries catch up with the higher level of development reached

elsewhere. Boublil proposes to achieve the same effect by initial subsidies.

175. Ibid., pp. 77-80.
176. Ibid., p. 52.
177. Patrick Viveret, "Débat avec Michel Rocard," *Faire* (September 1976); and Rocard, "La gauche et les pouvoirs," *Bulletin ACADI* (January-February 1978).
178. J.-M. Quatrepoint in *Le Monde*, September 25, 1981.
179. See note 166 above; also Jacques Delors interview in *Le Nouvel Observateur*, October 24, 1981.
180. The image of Renault as a successful car manufacturer has been attacked lately; critics claimed especially that Renault was not nearly as profitable and did not pay as much in taxes as its main competitor, Peugeot. See for example André Fourçans in The *Wall Street Journal*, November 18, 1981. In fact, however, Renault paid its shareholder (the state) quite well, though more in form of interest on capital advances rather than in dividends, but the difference is only formal. Also, Renault expanded more successfully than Peugeot. C. Baudelaire in *Le Point*, November 23, 1981.
181. Interview with Pierre Dreyfus, *L'Expansion*, November 6, 1981.
182. Fifty-one percent of the SNCF are owned by the state; 36 percent by the Banque Rothschild (which until its nationalization in 1982 was private), and 13 percent by the Groupe d'assurances de Paris. The private shareholders never exerted any control under this arrangement, and most people actually do not know that the state is not sole owner. Michel Rocard, *Parler vrai* (Paris: Le Seuil, 1979), pp. 145-46.
183. F.-O. Giesbert in *Le Nouvel Observateur*, September 12, 1981.
184. This can be done under Article 61 of the French Constitution.
185. J.-M. Quatrepoint and Ph. Boucher in *Le Monde*, January 19, 1982. For details of the decision, see *Le Monde* (weekly edition), January 14, 1982.
186. The two main steel producers, Usinor and Sacilor, had been nationalized earlier; this did not cause much controversy.

187. The figures quoted in the French press vary somewhat as to the exact dimensions. See J.-M. Quatrepoint in *Le Monde*, February 13, 1982; but also Philippe Labarde, ibid., February 19, 1982; and ibid., April 19, 1982.

188. Guy Sorman in the *Wall Street Journal*, May 19, 1982.

189. Georges Perrineau, "L'ampleur actuelle du champ des nationalisations," *Revue politique et parlementaire* (July 1981), p. 62. Much of the investment of these firms took place in the energy sector (nuclear energy, in particular), which is so capital-intensive that its contribution to employment is minimal, in fact probably negative. On the evolution of public and private investment, see Jacky Fayolle, "Le comportement d'investissement depuis 1974," *Economie et statistique* (November 1980), p. 23.

190. Roger Priouret in *Le Nouvel Observateur*, March 6, 1982. Lack of investment capital was made up in part by rising indebtedness to banks. Whereas in 1974 debts in industry were about four times as large as annual profits, by 1982 they were about ten times as large. Priouret stressed an obvious point (but one that the Socialists seemed to ignore until Mitterrand brought up this subject in his press conference of June 1982); namely, that an improvement of this situation also called for a fiscal penalty on real estate investment. Some of the defenders of a capitalist order in France are prepared to admit this deficiency of private investment in industry; however, they may explain it on different grounds. Jacques de Fouchier, one of the leading private bankers, argued in 1977 that the lack of investment was due to the fear of expropriation (without full compensation) created by the Common Program of the Left. Jacques de Fouchier in *1978. Si la gauche l'emportait*, pp. 66 and 68.

191. R. Priouret in *Le Nouvel Observateur*, September 12, 1981, and Dreyfus interview with *Le Point*, October 5, 1981.

192. J.-M. Quatrepoint in *Le Monde* (weekly edition), August 18, 1981. The same point was made by Japanese critics of American capitalism—that considerations of short-term profitability were an obstacle to an intelligent industrial strategy.

193. Moussa, himself sympathetic to the French Left, thought that he had assurances that the international division of Paribas would not be nationalized. When the government proceeded to na-

tionalize it anyhow, he helped with arranging a stock transfer that made Paribas lose control over its subsidiary in Switzerland. The operation was not then illegal, but Moussa had misrepresented his activities to the government; he also was clearly subverting the policy of the government. F.-O. Giesbert in *Le Nouvel Observateur*, November 14, 1981; *Le Monde*, October 28, November 2 and 3, 1981. Paribas recovered some of its stake (but not a majority) after secret negotiations conducted by Jacques de Fouchier; *Le Nouvel Observateur*, December 26, 1981, and *Les Echos*, February 11, 1982.

194. Mitterrand in his press conference of September 1981, *Le Monde* (weekly edition), September 24, 1981.

195. F.-O. Giesbert in *Le Nouvel Observateur*, September 26, 1981.

196. F.-O. Giesbert in *Le Nouvel Observateur*, October 17, 1981 (on Rocard); Delors interviews, ibid., October 24, 1981.

197. Dreyfus interview with *L'Expansion*, November 6, 1981.

198. "Reorienting the economy" is the title of a chapter heading in *Projet socialiste* (Paris: Club socialiste du livre, 1980), a programmatic statement "for the 1980s."

199. In some cases, the technical expertise seemed to have priority (thus Jean Gandois remained at Rhône-Poulenc, despite violent attacks by the CGT). He resigned however in the summer of 1982, disagreeing with governmental policy.

200. Philippe Labarde in *Le Monde*, February 19, 1982.

201. Jacques Jublin in *Les Echos*, February 17, 1982.

202. Jean Auroux in *Paris-Match*, March 5, 1982; also Pierre Dreyfus, interview in *Les Echos*, February 18, 1982.

203. *Le Nouvel Observateur*, April 3, 1982.

204. F.-O. Giesbert and Jacques Mornand in *Le Nouvel Observateur*, May 22, 1982.

205. Véronique Maurus in *Le Monde*, March 20, 1982. (The state took 51 percent of the stock.)

206. It seems that Mitterrand would like to see a further increase of the public sector, particularly if the recent nationalizations turn out to be successful. Roger Priouret, *Le Nouvel Observateur*, December 12, 1981.

207. *Les Echos*, February 18, 1982; and Giesbert and Mornand in *Le Nouvel Observateur*, May 22, 1982.

208. Jean-Michel Quatrepoint in *Le Monde*, April 22, 1982 and *Les Echos*, April 6, 1982.

209. Roger Priouret, *Le Nouvel Observateur*, April 3, 1982; Giesbert and Mornand, *Le Nouvel Observateur*, May 22, 1982.

210. Christian Pierret (Socialist deputy and general rapporteur for the budget) in *Le Nouvel Observateur*, June 5, 1982.

211. *Les Echos*, February 18, 1982.

212. See footnote 291.

213. François Renard in *Le Monde*, February 18, 1982; *Les Echos*, April 22, 1982.

214. *Les Echos*, September 16, 1982.

215. Delors interview with *Le Nouvel Observateur*, October 24, 1981.

216. *Le Monde*, September 17, 1981 (citing Mauroy).

217. The main reason may not be a reluctance to cooperate as much as the deteriorating cash situation of the firms. *Les Echos*, February 8, 1982.

218. *Les Echos*, February 26, 1982.

219. *Wall Street Journal*, February 11, 1982.

220. Dominique Audibert and Denis Jeambar in *Le Point*, April 19, 1982; Philippe Labarde in *Le Monde*, April 19, 1982.

221. Dreyfus interview in *Le Point*, October 5, 1981; J. P. Adine and D. Willot in *Le Point*, December 7, 1981; and P. Lamm in *Les Echos*, January 13, 1982.

222. François Renard in *Le Monde*, December 3, 1981.

223. In the textile and clothing industry, the government took over—for a limited period of time—part of the social welfare contributions, a measure that is important for this particularly labor-intensive sector. It was done on the condition that the firms concerned invest and hire new personnel. *Les Echos*, February 8, 1982. For the other industries see J.-P. Adine and D. Willot in *Le Point*, December 7, 1981; F. Grosrichard in *Le Monde*, December 10, 1981.

224. Adine in *Le Point*, January 18, 1982.

225. *Le Monde*, August 27, 1982; Chevènement in *Les Echos*, September 21, 1982.

226. Adrian Sinfield, "Poverty and inequality in France," in Vic George and Roger Lawson, eds., *Poverty and Inequality in Common Market Countries* (London: Routledge and Kegan Paul, 1980), pp. 92-95.

227. See, in particular, Marguerite Perrot, "Le pouvoir d'achat des salaires," *Economie et statistique* (January 1980), pp. 41-52.

228. It affected only 8 percent of all wage-earners directly (by contrast, the 35.1 percent minimum wage increase granted in 1968 affected 12.5 percent of the wage-earners). *Le Monde,* November 20, 1981, citing a study of the Ministry of Labor, published November 18.

229. *Les Echos,* February 15 and 24, 1982; *Le Monde,* June 15, 1982.

230. *Le Monde,* February 27, 1982.

231. See below, under unemployment.

232. *Le Monde,* February 10, 1982.

233. *Les Echos,* February 19, and April 30, 1982; Mitterrand in his press conference of June 9, 1982.

234. M. Roy in *Le Point,* August 31, 1981; and *Le Monde* (weekly edition), October 1, 1981. Mitterrand had announced that the business property would not be taxed.

235. Jacques Mornand, *Le Nouvel Observateur,* February 27, 1982.

236. *Le Monde,* March 3, 1982. Mitterrand in his press conference of June 9, 1982 announced measures to encourage formation of risk capital.

237. Olivier Marchand and Jean-Pierre Revoil, "Emploi et chômage: bilan fin 1980," *Economie et statistique* (February 1981).

238. *Le Point,* July 27, 1981; goal reasserted by Mauroy, *Le Monde,* September 17, 1981.

239. The decree procedure (article 38 of the French Constitution) was resorted primarily to speed things up. *Le Monde,* November 20, 1981; *Le Monde,* February 8, 1982.

240. Discussion between Christian Goux (one of Mitterrand's economic advisers) and Raymond Soubie (former adviser for Raymond Barre) on the reduction of working time, *Le Point,* January 18, 1982.

241. Jean-Pierre Dumont in *Le Monde*, February 13, 1982.
242. *Les Echos*, February 11 and 12, 1982.
243. Dumont, *Le Monde*, February 13, 1982; and A. Laurens, *Le Monde*, February 15, 1982.
244. *Les Echos*, April 13, 1982. However, they rarely led to job creation.
245. Claude Sales, *Le Point*, February 15, 1982; Jacques Julliard, *Le Nouvel Observateur*, February 27, 1982.
246. Dominique Audibert and Denis Jeambar, *Le Point*, April 19, 1982.
247. *Les Echos*, January 20, 1982.
248. *Le Monde*, May 4, 1982.
249. Mauroy announced such a plan in September 1981; see *Le Monde*, September 17, 1981.
250. Michel Albert interviewed in *Le Nouvel Observateur*, June 5, 1982.
251. In an IFOP survey of 35-60 year olds, conducted in March 1982, 84 percent were favorable to lowering the retirement age to 60; only 4 percent were opposed. Survey published in *Le Point*, April 5, 1982.
252. Claude Sales, *Le Point*, April 5, 1982; Jean-Pierre Dumont in *Le Monde*, March 26, 1982; *Les Echos*, March 12, 1982.
253. Patrick Artus, Henri Sterdyniak and Pierre Villa, "Investissement, emploi, et fiscalité," *Economie et statistique* (November 1980).
254. In France, contributions by employers and wage-earners financed (in 1977) 81.5 percent of all social protection; in Italy, 71.3 percent; in Germany, 69.9 percent; and in Britain, 52.8 percent. Ibid., p. 121.
255. Ibid., p. 119.
256. The authors of the article propose an 18.5 percent tax on investment, with the proceeds of which they would finance a reduction of Social Security contributions by 5 points. They say that this would increase jobs by 300 thousand to 400 thousand over six years, and increase production by 1-1.5 percent. Ibid., p. 115.
257. The beneficiaries were around 300 thousand in number. *Les Echos*, January 19, 1982. In the past, the *Pacte National pour l'emploi* had often subsidized jobs that were not permanent; this

was supposed to change. Roger Priouret, *Le Nouvel Observateur*, August 22, 1981.

258. *Les Echos*, February 8, 1982.

259. *Le Monde*, March 26, 1982.

260. *Les Echos*, April 16, 1982.

261. *Le Monde*, May 7, 1982.

262. On the *lois Auroux*, see interview with Delors, *Le Nouvel Observateur*, October 24, 1981; A. Laurens in *Le Monde*, October 17, 1981; Roger Priouret in *Le Nouvel Observateur*, April 30, 1982; Kathleen Evin, ibid., May 8, 1982; and *Les Echos*, September 16, 1982.

263. *Plan intérimaire. Stratégie pour deux ans, 1982-1983* (Paris: La documentation française, 1981), pp. 207-209 and 213; *Le Point*, August 3, 1982; *Le Monde*, September 30, October 1 and 9, 1981; *Le Nouvel Observateur*, October 3 and 17, 1981.

264. This view was expressed regularly in the conservative newspapers such as *Le Figaro;* e.g. May 2-3, 1981.

265. The famous *accords Matignon* (1936) and *accords de Grenelle* (1968).

266. *Le Monde* (weekly edition), January 7, 1982.

267. *Le Monde*, March 16, 1982.

268. *Joint Statement by the Socialist Party and French Communist Party*, June 23, 1981.

269. C. Mital in *L'Expansion*, January 23, 1981; C.-F. Jullien and T. Pfister in *Le Nouvel Observateur*, March 2, 1981.

270. C.-F. Jullien in *Le Nouvel Observateur*, March 9 and March 30, 1981.

271. J. Roy in *Le Monde*, October 16, 1981.

272. J.-P. Dumont in *Le Monde*, January 8, 1982; D. Audibert in *Le Point*, January 18, 1982.

273. Confusion was still evident in May 1982. Denis Jeambar, *Le Point*, May 24, 1982.

274. Jean-Yves Lhomeau, *Le Monde*, June 22, 1982.

275. Jean-Yves Lhomeau, *Le Monde*, May 6, 1982.

276. Kathleen Evin, *Le Nouvel Observateur*, May 8, 1982.

277. *Le Monde*, May 25, 1982; Jean-Marie Colombani, *Le Monde*, June 4, 1982.

278. Kathleen Evin, *Le Nouvel Observateur*, April 3, 1982.

279. *Motion nationale d'orientation,* Valence Party Congress, para. III(2) and V (4) (b).

280. Alain Rollat in *Le Monde,* March 17, 1982. The Socialist Party responded by saying that the government should show more coherence in its policy; Jean-Yves Lhomeau, *Le Monde,* April 6, 1982. Also around this time, Pierre Joxe (leader of the Socialist deputies and a neo-Marxist himself) made a strong attack on Prime Minister Mauroy. Franz-Oliver Giesbert, *Le Nouvel Observateur,* April 30, 1982.

281. Jean-Pierre Dumont, *Le Monde,* February 8, 1982.

282. Georges Sarre, "Les syndicats ne jouent pas le jeu," *Le Nouvel Observateur,* June 5, 1982.

283. Thus, the CGT is strongly in favor of the nationalizations (something that meets with doubts from CFDT and Force ouvrière) and was long opposed to any austerity, in particular also to wage reductions on the occasion of the 39-hour week. Differences extend to all major areas of change, in particular the *lois Auroux.*

284. Thus it was de Gaulle who contained the French nationalists and their ambitions for Algeria and Nixon who checked anti-Communism as an obstacle to détente.

285. William L. Shirer, *Collapse of the Third Republic,* (New York: Simon and Schuster, 1969) pp. 160-65.

286. Here the contrast with 1936 was particularly strong. The capital drain started between the election and Blum's access to power; Blum then hoped to bring it to a halt by promising that he would respect liberal economic principles (that is, not impose exchange controls).

287. Announced by Budget Minister Laurent Fabius on September 30, 1981, to take effect immediately. *Le Monde* (weekly edition) October 1, 1981. (Fabius took no chances—he made the announcement during a press conference, but waited with this particular item until 6 P.M., when the banks were closed.)

288. Maurice Roy in *Le Point,* May 11, 1981; J.-M. Quatrepoint in *Le Monde,* May 16, 1981. The phenomenon was implicitly recognized by Yvon Gattaz later on; *Les Echos,* January 26, 1982.

289. Philippe Labarde in *Le Monde,* November 18, 1981; Maurice Roy in *Le Point,* November 23, 1981.

118   The Politics of Economic Policy

290. Roger Priouret in *Le Nouvel Observateur,* November 28 and December 12, 1981. He cites specifically a bulletin from the Employers' Organization (the CNPF) dated November 1981; it did not in a single word mention the expansion that was under way, but gave all the reasons why firms should not invest, sometimes citing questionable data.

291. The document adopted at Valence spoke of the "class enemy" and of the need to carry the class struggle into business enterprises. Valence Party Congress, *Motion nationale d'orientation,* para. III and V. Mauroy and Mitterrand expressed their disagreement; Danièle Molho in *Le Point,* November 30, 1981; *Le Monde,* December 9, 1981.

292. *Le Nouvel Economiste,* December 21, 1981.

293. F.-O. Giesbert in *Le Nouvel Observateur,* November 14, 1981; *Le Monde,* October 28, November 2 and 3, 1981.

294. Shirer, *Collapse of the Third Republic,* p. 324.

295. *Les Echos,* April 8 and 9, 1982.

296. Yvon Gattaz in *Les Echos,* March 29, 1982.

297. Jean Daniel, *Le Nouvel Observateur,* December 5, 1981.

298. Pierre Locardel in *Les Echos,* April 21, 1982.

299. *Les Echos,* April 23, 1982.

300. Undoubtedly the authoritarian structures of many business firms have shaped the mindsets of union leaders as well as of employers; it is not inappropriate to expect problems of transition.

301. *Le Monde* (weekly edition), January 7, 1982.

302. Irène Allier in *Le Nouvel Observateur,* October 3, 1981; Bernard Stasi interview in *Paris-Match,* January 15, 1982; *Les Echos,* February 17, 1982; and *Le Point,* February 22, 1982.

303. *Les Echos,* April 6 and 8, 1982; *Le Monde,* June 12, 1982.

304. *Le Monde* (weekly edition), January 7, 1982.

305. Geneviève Galey in *Le Point,* May 25, 1981.

306. André Passeron in *Le Monde,* July 20, 1981; report on Chirac press conference, *Le Monde,* October 7, 1981; and Passeron in *Le Monde,* January 26, 1982.

307. Georges Mamy, *Le Nouvel Observateur,* February 13, 1982.

308. *Le Figaro-magazine,* April 9, 1982.

309. Georges Mamy, *Le Nouvel Observateur,* May 15, 1982.
310. RPR militants were more cautious. *Les Echos,* September 27, 1982.
311. Laurent Zecchini, *Le Monde,* May 31, 1982. The most likely procedure to be applied would be Article 49 (3) of the Constitution, by which the government can impose a law unless a motion of censure is voted against it.
312. Thus, Giscard stated that he approved of the regionalization reform, and even of the fifth week of vacations (G. Mamy, *Le Nouvel Observateur,* June 5, 1982); Barre stated his approval of the natural gas contract with the Soviet Union and praised the Mauroy government for its policy of wage discipline (*Les Echos,* February 1, 1982). Still they both thought that the Socialists would fail in the end.
313. Interview with Claude Labbé, *Paris-Match,* March 5, 1982.
314. Both SOFRES (September 10-16) and IFOP (September 14-20) surveys showed more negative than positive evaluations. Both cited in *Les Echos,* September 27, 1982.
315. In the last three regional elections (1976, 1979, 1982), the Socialists made continuous progress; the other groups of the Left declined, however.
316. Jean-Yves Lhomeau, *Le Monde,* April 6, 1982.
317. Franz-Olivier Giesbert, *Le Nouvel Observateur,* March 27, 1982.
318. Roger Priouret, *Le Nouvel Observateur,* May 8, 1982.

About the Author

Volkmar Lauber is professor of political science at the University of Salzburg, Austria. He was chairman of the Department of Government at West Virginia Wesleyan College from 1977 to 1982 and visiting professor at The Johns Hopkins University Bologna Center in 1979–1980. He received his Ph.D. in political science from the University of North Carolina at Chapel Hill and his LL.M. from the Harvard Law School. He has published numerous articles in European and American publications.